RHYTHM MAKERS

RHYTHM MAKERS

The Drumming Legends of Nashville in Their Own Words

Tony Artimisi

ROWMAN & LITTLEFIELD
Lanham • Boulder • New York • London

Published by Rowman & Littlefield
A wholly owned subsidiary of The Rowman & Littlefield Publishing Group, Inc.
4501 Forbes Boulevard, Suite 200, Lanham, Maryland 20706
www.rowman.com

Unit A, Whitacre Mews, 26-34 Stannary Street, London SE11 4AB

British Library Cataloguing in Publication Information Available

Library of Congress Cataloging-in-Publication Data

Artimisi, Tony, author.
Rhythm makers : the drumming legends of Nashville in their own words / Tony Artimisi.
pages cm
Includes index.
ISBN 978-1-4422-4011-7 (hardcover : alk. paper) — ISBN 978-1-4422-4012-4 (ebook)
1. Drummers (Musicians)—Interviews. 2. Popular music—Tennessee—Nashville—History and criticism. 3. Bayers, Eddie—Interviews. 4. Kroon, Jerry—Interviews. 5. Malone, Kenny—Interviews. 6. Roady, Tom—Interviews. 7. Wells, Tommy—Interviews. I. Title.
ML399.A78 2015
786.9'164092276855—dc23
2014047261

Printed in the United States of America

To my wife: the credit is as much yours as mine.

CONTENTS

FOREWORD

Waldo LaTowsky

Eddie Bayers, Kenny Malone, Jerry Kroon, Tom Roady, and Tommy Wells. These were some of the most influential drummers in the music business when I moved to Nashville in the late eighties, and it was relatively easy to hear them playing in clubs or holding clinics in one of the local stores. Unlike Larrie Londin (who, sadly, passed away years before Tony Artimisi began this interview project), I wasn't familiar with them, so I wasn't in awe of their talents.

Until I heard them play. To hear each of those Nashville greats playing with other incredible musicians in a relaxed nonconcert setting changed my perception of music in general, and my concept of drumming in particular, in ways that remain with me to this day. Whether speaking or just playing, each of them imparted enough information to make every performance a master class in the art of making music. As session drummers, their subtle and masterful contributions to country and pop music cannot be overstated, though that same status guarantees they're not well known outside the industry.

There were many clubs with live music, so hungry musicians went out every night to hear what they could, and in many cases were well rewarded for the effort. The great bass player Victor Wooten might be playing along with the noted violinist ("fiddle player" at the time) Mark O'Connor, and perhaps Vince Gill, Ray Flacke, or Brent Mason, also. Even the lesser-known players were amazing. At the same club where I saw Wooten and O'Connor, I heard a drummer who was working hard not to draw attention to himself but whom I couldn't ignore because of the masterful way he played the hi-hats. The tunes and other players were excellent, but the way this drummer laid down a subtle but insistent and continually bubbling pulse was something I had never heard before. What a groove!

It was Jerry Kroon. I approached him during a break, told him how amazing I thought he was, and he responded with the same humility I came to recognize as a standard Nashville trait, going so far as to say *he envied me* because I was new, fresh, and could play any style I wanted with whomever I wanted, whereas he was primarily a studio player and, as such, was limited to certain types of music. I obviously didn't agree with that analysis, but he offered to show me by inviting me to a major recording session. I couldn't believe it, but a few days later I was on Music Row, in a studio with a group of Nashville's finest session musicians.

Jerry introduced me to a few of them, there was much hustle and bustle, and at one point in our conversation Jerry said, "Hang on a minute," picked up a notebook, and started scribbling something. There was some music playing for a few minutes (I hadn't noticed because I was concentrating on what he was saying), and then Jerry returned to the conversation. I asked him what he'd done, and he said he'd charted the song so he could record it! I'd never heard of such a thing and told him I couldn't believe he could do that so quickly— having played the song only once—and he assured me I'd be able to do the same thing after I'd been in town awhile. He was correct about that; the Nashville Number System is a musical shorthand every Nashville musician perfects, and it has spread far beyond its Tennessee roots. Jerry then excused himself, walked into the drum booth, and laid down his part perfectly, with the same understated grace I'd first heard live.

People had been telling me about Kenny Malone and his track record of country hits, so when I heard Kenny was giving a rare clinic, I arrived early and sat in the front row, eager to absorb a master's knowledge of being a session drummer.

Obviously, I didn't know Kenny.

We all sat on the floor of D.O.G. Percussion, a legendary drum shop owned by Larrie Londin's wife, Debbie Gallant, and waited for the introduction of the main man. While we were waiting, a guy who looked like he might work behind the counter at Western Auto started walking around the room striking a small finger cymbal with a pen. Of course, it was Kenny, setting the mood for what was to follow—one of the most unusual *nonclinics* I ever attended. He spoke on a wide range of subjects, clearly avoided anything so mundane as "How to Make a Living Playing the Drums in Nashville" or "How to Play the Beats You'll Need to Know to Succeed," and talked about his recent foray into throwing pots. He had taken pottery lessons so he could make his own drums, and he played one of his creations at the clinic, along with the man I grew to know as his partner in sound, the great percussionist, drum maker, and drum historian Sam Bacco. The drum Kenny played had three heads—one on top and two others of different sizes distributed along the sides. I've still never seen anything similar to it (though I saw him use it on gigs in clubs). Musically, it was a wonderful day full of exploring odd sounds and examining dynamics.

I'd gone from a real, very specific example of how the studio music business works to something more resembling a philosophical, almost Socratic method of pursuing knowledge, regardless of its possible application to the world of country music. And that was reinforced when I approached Kenny asking him for lessons. His response: "No lessons. Breakfast."

He explained that he was bored with the concept of "me teacher, you student" but that he welcomed friendly conversation. For years, these breakfasts were forums where they (Kenny, Sam, and a revolving cast of others) discussed (I mostly listened) such things as how to get the perfect heartbeat sound. At one point, they concluded it required muscle and gristle to duplicate the sound effectively, so the solution *must* be to suspend a chicken carcass—just the right size and weight chicken carcass, of course—in a pool, whack it with a stick, and record the result. This is a very debatable point, but it could be said that Kenny Malone attempted more strange sounds and used more strange non-instruments as instruments than anyone in Nashville history. Like most of his friends, I treasure Kenny Malone, but I realized then I was going to need to search elsewhere for more reality-based information on how to become a successful Nashville drummer.

I spent most of my free time searching out new and interesting players, and one evening I came across a man who was to become a wonderful friend through the years.

This was the incomparable Tommy Wells, who has sadly passed away but remains one of the most solid drummers I have ever heard.

And that night, Tommy taught me a lesson using a trick I've never heard anyone else use. He *never* took a fill or wavered from the surging backbeat he'd set up. And I realized why it was so masterful. Because it never changed (except dynamically, and he was a master at that), it communicated on a level beneath what the audience was consciously aware of, one that created an emotional tension that could not be perceived or achieved any other way.

Tommy Wells's license plate, immediately recognizable to Nashville musicians, was "2 AND 4," a perfect indication of just how solid his playing was. Tommy and I became friends and continued meeting through the years for long conversations on the nature of swing and studio history. Tommy Wells will always be greatly missed as a man and musician, but also because he had an encyclopedic knowledge of recorded music, drums (acoustic and electronic), and music history (pop especially), and he was happy to share it with anyone who would ask.

Though it was one of the first events I saw in Nashville, I've saved it for last because it involves the remaining two subjects of the book. Shortly after I moved, I attended a clinic at one of the local studios featuring Eddie Bayers, who had been highly recommended as someone to see. Eddie was, and remains, one of the biggest session drummers in the business. He arrived, mentioned he'd just invited a friend of his to sit in on the clinic, and introduced percussionist Tom Roady. The two of them played and I couldn't determine who was more compelling to listen to, Eddie or Tom. They each played with such confidence and ease, and their combined groove was all the more infectious because it was spontaneous. It was captivating in terms of entertainment and information. After the clinic, I introduced myself to both of them and went home and took *Percussion* off my business card (it was too late to remove *Drums*, though I considered it).

I took it off my card because Tom Roady showed me what being a percussionist was about. Whether it was that first meeting or the innumerable times we spent together as friends later, Roady was always teaching me how to sweeten a groove. He became one of the best friends I've had, and I miss him every day, but this is not the place to mourn him. It's the place to celebrate his contributions to music, and the incredible, bubbling warmth and humor that drove not only his personality but also his playing. Though there are certainly other worthy percussionists in Nashville history (the aforementioned Bacco and Farrell Morris among them), it could be said that Roady (few people called him Tom) was the one who brought a pop sensibility to Nashville country music in a way that helped it break its seemingly regional barriers at just the right time. It could also be said that Roady will always be one of the most entertaining players to watch. No one who ever saw him will forget that huge smile that spread across his face the moment the music began. And, like Tommy Wells, Tom Roady was loved by all the musicians who came after him because he was not only personally generous with his advice and critiques but because he had an incredible knowledge of who played with whom, who recorded what and where, and how people arrived at sounds.

It's impossible to mention Nashville drummers without including Eddie Bayers. His discography is huge, and what Tony has written serves his story well. My contact with him began at that session and continued on through clinics he would hold. Unlike the first one, Eddie's clinics didn't usually feature a lot of playing, but often concentrated more on Q-and-A sessions, due to that large discography and the tremendous amount of knowledge he has about drums, sound, and achieving the perfect groove. As Tony touches on in his interview, Eddie has a deep piano background, which could contribute to the reason so many artists think of him as the perfect complement for *the song*. To learn the Nashville style means learning Eddie Bayers's drum parts. For many, he's the gold standard, though the industry is full of great players and more appear each day. I've had other musicians who've played with him say he just "has it," and watching him from backstage play live made a believer out of me. I saw him concentrate on the pulse so intently before he counted off the tune that the band was completely together in the groove *before the song began*. That's control, and dedication.

Nashville is the songwriting capital of the world, first and foremost, and it revolves around artists, not musicians. The task of session musicians is to contribute in ways that complement that hierarchy and move beyond it to communicate the emotion, enhance the music, and help it change and evolve with the times.

Each of the players featured here added elements to the music that the producers and songwriters could never have imagined, and millions around the world have danced, laughed, and cried to the result. They may not be household names, and their art may not be immediately perceivable, but they couldn't be any more important to the process. *Rhythm Makers: The Drumming Legends of Nashville in Their Own Words* is a unique glimpse into the heart and soul of contemporary music, and we all owe Tony Artimisi a debt of gratitude for his effort.

ACKNOWLEDGMENTS

I would like to thank the following individuals for their support, contributions, and encouragement:

My wife and children for waiting patiently for this project to be finished. I love you very much.

My parents for supporting my musical ambition and tolerating a very noisy house for a lot of years.

Waldo LaTowsky has been my sounding board throughout this project. His experiences with the drummers featured and his knowledge of the Nashville community have been invaluable.

The wives of Tom Roady and Tommy Wells: Melanie Roady and Carolyn Breda. I am heartbroken that Tom and Tommy didn't see this project through to completion but am so happy that their legacy lives on. You have been so great through this process. Thank you from the bottom of my heart. They were amazing men and are dearly missed.

Eddie Bayers Jr., Jerry Kroon, and Kenny Malone. What more can be said? I'm still shocked that you agreed to the interviews. You guys did what you always do: knocked the ball out of the park! Your collective efforts to deliver the best possible product, on time, and with great attitudes demonstrated to me why you were all so successful for so long.

Jamie Tate, owner/operator of the Rukkus Room recording studio, for letting us use your tracking room for the interviews.

Jon and Amy Lechner for your hospitality and friendship over the years.

Andrew Shreve, Jace McDonald, and Arturo Gil of Paiste Inc.; Rick DeJonge, Joseph Hibbs, Jeff Mulvihill, and Chris Hankes at Mapex Drums/Majestic Percussion; and Neil Grover and Dave Share at Grover Pro Percussion. Thank you for your support.

The faculty and staff of Winston-Salem State University.

Bennett Graff, senior editor at Rowman & Littlefield, for your guidance and patience throughout this project.

INTRODUCTION

Nashville, Tennessee, is hailed as "Music City, USA." The degree to which music saturates the local culture is staggering. Every year, hundreds if not thousands of musically gifted people relocate to the city in hopes of fulfilling their dreams of success in the music business, and with good reason: the city's legacy as a major musical market extends back nearly a century to the early days of *The Grand Ole Opry* in the 1920s.

The Grand Ole Opry began as a regional radio show called *The WSM Barn Dance* on WSM Radio in 1925. It featured a variety of acts performing what is regarded as some of the earliest contemporary country music. As was common for the era, radio stations were often the locations of recording facilities. This was true for WSM, and some of Nashville's earliest popular recordings for record labels were created at WSM Studios A and B. *The WSM Barn Dance* became known as *The Grand Ole Opry* in 1927.

Nashville's music industry expanded greatly beginning in 1939, when NBC began broadcasting WSM's *The Grand Ole Opry* nationwide. In response to the increased reach that network radio stations provided, many music businesses relocated their regional offices to the major broadcast areas to focus on maximizing their listening audiences. The music scenes in Nashville, Los Angeles, Chicago, and New York benefited greatly from this phenomenon and are still the primary American music centers.

As the Nashville music industry continued to develop around a deep pool of songwriters, charismatic entertainers, and musicians, the music industry primarily based their offices in a two-to-three-mile area of downtown that became known as Music Row on 16th and 17th Avenues South. The types of businesses located on Music Row include record companies, publishing companies, management offices, the American Federation of Musicians Local #257, recording studios, and performance rights organizations. No other city in the United States contains as many music-industry businesses in such a concentrated area. Metaphorically, the feet of music industry royalty regularly walk the streets of Music Row.

The revenue generated by all of the businesses on Music Row helped improve the quality of the recording facilities, which were quickly growing in number. A strong market creates competition, and the best and busiest studios continuously upgraded their equipment as the technology became more sophisticated. The abundance of state-of-the-art facilities attracted artists and record producers from a variety of areas and genres. Although Nashville is commonly viewed as a country music town, major albums by artists that one wouldn't necessarily associate with that type of music are regularly recorded there. The client lists of popular facilities include Bob Dylan, Simon & Garfunkel, Roy Orbison, Sting, Elton John, and, more recently, Kesha, Maroon 5, Michael Bublé, Justin Bieber, Bon Jovi, the Red Hot Chili Peppers, and the Black Eyed Peas. As one would expect, the caliber of musician who can successfully navigate such a wide variety of styles is very high.

A "recording session" and, more simply, a "session" are the terms used to describe the time reserved in a recording studio. The American Federation of Musicians (AFM), the labor union that works to ensure fair wages and working conditions for instrumentalists, has negotiated rates for the different types of projects necessary to take a song from conception to mass-marketed completion. A recording session is three hours in length, includes a ten-minute break each hour, and places limits on the amount of recorded music that can be completed in each session. In addition, the AFM has negotiated pension contributions, deducts taxes from musicians' paychecks, and provides numerous other benefits to its members. Some examples of different session types are TV/jingle (television or commercial music), demonstration or demo, limited pressing, and master.

A demonstration recording session is the classification for recordings that will not be sold or mastered. These are used by songwriters and publishing companies to create recordings of songs that showcase a song idea for presentation to a record producer or recording artist. If the demo is successful, the artist or producer will license the song for placement on an album. At this point, a master recording session will be booked, which is the designation used to describe the session leading to a major album released by a record label. The pay scale, or "scale rate," for master sessions are higher than the other session pay scales.

A recording session musician, or session musician, is an instrumentalist hired to create the backing tracks that support the songwriter or recording artist. There are numerous paths one can take to build and sustain a career as a session musician, as will be discussed by the interviewees in this book, but there are some common traits that aid success in this field. Aside from the obvious requirement to be a technically proficient performer, it is necessary to be quickly creative, have a strong ability to remember songs after hearing them (retention), be able to adapt to somebody else's artistic vision, and routinely perform under high pressure while maintaining a positive attitude.

The process of introducing a new song to the session musicians prior to recording is well established. The song is played by the songwriter or the demo recording of the song is played for the musicians, who follow along with prepared sheet music charts created by the session leader. The Nashville Number System (NNS) was devised as a method to quickly create charts. It follows the same philosophy that figured bass systems use in traditional music theory—scale degrees are assigned a number that corresponds to the chord and chord quality typical of each scale degree in the key signature. That may sound difficult, but it is elegantly simple once a musician becomes fluent in the method.

The NNS solved a few problems. The Nashville office was historically one of the few AFM locations that did not require musicians to be able to read traditionally notated sheet music to become members. There are no notes or rhythms to read using the NNS. This allowed musicians who may have been technically proficient and creative players but not the strongest notation readers to quickly learn and create parts for songs. Additionally, since the NNS deals with scale degrees and not notation, songs can be transposed to any key without needing to be rewritten. This is very convenient if a vocalist wants to perform a song in a higher key to better suit his or her vocal range. The only edit to the chart the musicians have to make in this scenario is to scratch out a "C" (hypothetical key) on the chart and write "E ♭ " (the new key). The chord relationships, and the rest of the arrangement, remain the same.

Once the song is heard, the musicians and record producer will often discuss any ideas, confusing parts, or changes with the goal of getting the best possible version of the song. When a general consensus is reached, the players move to their instruments, make changes to the settings to fit the song's style, and generally prepare to perform the song. If everybody looks to be ready, the record producer will tell the musicians to run through it. This initial run-through will almost certainly be recorded in case "lightning strikes" and the song is performed perfectly the first time. The first performances of a song generally have the most energy and feel of spontaneity, which get more difficult to maintain with successive attempts. With session musicians of this quality, it is a very real possibility that significant portions of the first run-through will be usable.

After the first run-through, there will be discussion about the tempo, key, and any ideas, questions, comments, or concerns. Once those items have been addressed, everybody will be ready to record the song. This will be considered the true "first take," and many session musicians pride themselves on completing their work on the first take with minimal mistakes to correct, if any. The amount of time that passes between hearing the song for the first time through completion of the first take could be as little as twenty minutes.

Work on the song will continue. There are a number of possibilities of what will happen next, including changing the arrangement or direction of the song if necessary. If the first take is acceptable, additional layers will often be added to embellish the arrangement until it reaches its finished form in this step of the recording phase. This is called "overdubbing." The vocalist will commonly record the final vocal performances after the instrumental tracks are completed. The album will then be ready for mixing and mastering in preparation for mass distribution.

The role of the session drummer has evolved over the years. While the drum set typically lays the foundation upon which the rest of a song is built in modern commercial music, traditional Nashville-based country music didn't include drums. The earliest percussive sounds in country music were created by a muted acoustic guitar. There were isolated instances of drums being played on *The Grand Ole Opry*, but the instrument was largely forbidden from the show for many years.

Farris Coursey became the first staff drummer hired at WSM in 1937 and performed on many of the country music recordings of the era. He used mostly a snare drum with brushes. Another drummer, whom many consider the most important drummer in Nashville history, began his Nashville music career in the early 1950s: Buddy Harman. He was a member of the famed "A Team" of session musicians, which included a rotating group of exceptional players. The rhythm section consisted of Harold Bradley (guitar), Hank Garland (guitar), Ray Edenton (guitar), Grady Martin (guitar), Bob Moore (bass guitar), Floyd Cramer (piano), Hargus "Pig" Robbins (piano), and Pete Drake (steel guitar). Harman is recognized as the drummer who facilitated the transition from quiet, brush-on-snare drumming to the full drum set on Nashville recordings with Elvis Presley, Roy Orbison, and other artists from the 1950s to the 1980s. This transition demonstrates the influence that rock 'n' roll and other heavier styles had on country music as the genre developed.

Larrie Londin is also very important in Nashville's drum legacy. As will be detailed by the drummers in this book, Londin had a helping hand in the careers of many of the drummers fortunate enough to cross his path. He was the unofficial leader of the drumming community throughout the 1980s. His drumming style opened up new possibilities for a country record. He also broke the stereotype that labeled Nashville drummers technically deficient with his virtuosity behind the drum set.

The five men interviewed for this book were contemporaries of Londin. Each has all of the qualities outlined above that successful session musicians must possess. Keeping that in mind, it is very interesting to see how each created a unique place in the Nashville drumming lexicon to sustain a lengthy and eclectic career.

Eddie Bayers Jr.'s career has been so successful and varied that it is difficult to summarize. His drumming has influenced a generation of players. He has an outstanding sense of time, feel, and finesse and is highly regarded for his ability to craft the right part for a song. Beyond that, he is a successful record producer, is former owner of a successful recording facility, and was even a staff writer for Acuff-Rose Music. His advanced business sense becomes apparent throughout the interview as he details the many areas of the industry in which he participated.

Starting his career in South Dakota, Jerry Kroon shows how a patient, calculated approach can be used to great success in the industry. His drumming appears on records by Willie Nelson, Dolly Parton, Ray Stevens, and many others. Kroon shares a wealth of information on maintaining good relationships with various personality types in music, how to approach the instrument in different playing situations, and his views on how to have a long, successful music career.

Kenny Malone has a musical voice that is unlike any other. His ability to create a unique musical statement has given producers great confidence in following his intuition wherever it may lead. He moved to Nashville after serving in the U.S. Navy and soon became one of the most popular drummers in town after Dobie Gray's "Drift Away" reached the top of the charts. Constantly experimenting with real and invented instruments, Malone was instrumental in the development of the "new grass" style, almost single-handedly defining the percussion technique of the genre.

Tom Roady details the particulars of his life and career beginning with his formative years in the St. Louis area. Music led him to Los Angeles, Las Vegas, and Muscle Shoals before he settled in Nashville and became one of the most important, and beloved, percussionists in the history of Music City, USA.

Tommy Wells began his career playing recording sessions in Motown on the weekends while flying to Boston to study at Berklee College of Music during the week. After touring the United States with several bands, and forming a friendship with Larrie Londin in the process, he moved to Nashville and almost immediately became an in-demand session player. His playing and equipment choices led to several changes in the style of drumming on country records. He also shares valuable insight into how jingle and soundalike sessions operate. The consummate sideman, Wells was one of Nashville's unsung heroes.

EDDIE BAYERS JR.

Eddie Bayers Jr. relocated many times while growing up as the son of a naval fighter pilot. He began his musical career working in New Jersey and California as a pianist and vocalist. He assessed that the opportunities were more suited to his preferences in Nashville, so he relocated in

1973. He soon auditioned for and was selected to play piano at the Carousel Club, alongside legendary drummer Larrie Londin, five nights a week.

From the outset of his arrival in Nashville, it seemed highly unlikely that Bayers, a pianist, would put together the kind of résumé as a drummer that would see him voted the Academy of Country Music's Drummer of the Year eleven times in a row and a sum total of thirteen times, inducted into Modern Drummer's *Hall of Fame, and listed as one of the Top Ten Session Drummers of All Time by* Drum! *magazine. However, the time he spent playing next to Larrie Londin inspired him to change instruments. His work ethic and musical sense quickly prepared him for a career as a working drummer. Recommendations to bandleaders from Londin got Bayers his first gigs, while his playing and professionalism took care of the rest.*

Throughout his career, he has added his talents to albums featuring some of the top artists in the last thirty years, including Sting, Lyle Lovett, Mark Knopfler, Steve Winwood, Garth Brooks, Uncle Kracker, Peter Cetera, Martina McBride, Willie Nelson, Michael Bolton, and Richard Marx. He was a songwriter for Acuff-Rose and wrote songs that were recorded by the Temptations, his own band the Players, Billy Joe Walker Jr., and John Jarvis. Bayers also owned a popular recording studio called the Money Pit, served on the board of directors for the National Academy of Recording Arts and Sciences (NARAS), and hosts and teaches seminars for Berklee College of Music.

Bayers's story is unique among this group of players because it doesn't begin behind the drums. In this interview, his determination, commitment to delivering a great performance, work ethic, and business savvy become apparent as he discusses the challenges, opportunities, and myriad forms of inspiration he encountered during his career.

A lot of your background was covered in the Country Music Hall of Fame interview, and I don't want to retread that ground. I do have a few questions about your college years before we spend the bulk of the time on the particulars of your professional career. How would you define your time in the Peralta College system (in California)?

It was more of a vocational experience—not so much academic. When I got there, a resident in the Peralta area could study a vocation at a community college for free. All the credits were transferable. They all had different facets. You could choose music theory, composition, or different areas of study. They had cosmetology and every other major.

I was a classically trained pianist, which I've talked about in other interviews. I was doing more of that than percussion. I already had a lot of piano background, but the college helped me get into the musical community.

So there were a lot of players studying there?

Oh, yeah. Once you get into the community, then the network starts. I was able to get work through that.

When did you start playing drums?

I was playing piano in high school. I imagine that you have experienced this. We always look at other instruments. I was interested, but I didn't think I was going to be a professional drummer.

I was also a vocalist. I sang on some projects too. I sang on a Paul Kantner and Grace Slick solo album apart from Jefferson Airplane. I also sang on Doug Clifford's record called *Cosmo*. He was in Creedence Clearwater Revival. That came out in the early 1970s [1972]. I also sang on Tom Fogerty's record. That's how I got involved with them.

Tom actually had an "outside the box" group that he put together. It was me on piano, Billy Vitt on drums, Merl Saunders on B-3, Tom played acoustic guitar, and Jerry Garcia played electric guitar.

What was Jerry Garcia like at that time?

He was a great guy. He never brought his ego with him. They were certainly at the top of everything at that point. You never felt any of that when playing with him. He just loved to play.

Was that before the Grateful Dead?

Oh, no, during. He was already a big name. Tom Fogerty was also an internationally known artist at the time through Creedence Clearwater Revival. This was something, just as we do, for them to do on the side. When you're in sessions every day, you get with other musicians and create a group that's outside of that to perform in different places.

That was all after you lived in Las Vegas, right?

Yes.

Wow, you were working with some big names as a young musician. What lessons do you feel you were learning from them?

I didn't look at it like it was an educational experience. It was a great opportunity to play and work into their chemistry. When I was with Tom Fogerty, the debacle that caused Creedence to break up happened.

Saul Zaentz, even though that group [Creedence Clearwater Revival] made him a hundred million dollars with Fantasy Records, always had a condescending attitude toward intellect. So he felt anything lower than that was not worth his respect, even though Creedence made him a lot of money. When he made his money, it seemed he felt that he could do what he wanted, which included buying Prestige Records—a jazz label (in 1971). Of course, his movies are well known, like *Amadeus* and *One Flew Over the Cuckoo's Nest*.

Still, he had this unbelievable dislike for John Fogerty, and John reciprocated. On top of that, there was tension between John and Tom, who were like true-life Smothers Brothers. Tom was always telling John that he [Tom] was a writer and singer, and John would tell him that they would try to record his work and present it to Saul. Tom then replied that he already did that and that Saul was going to give him his own deal. John tried to stop him because he knew what Saul's mission was. Tom did it anyway and it created fear in Doug Clifford and Stu Cook. So they got scared enough to accept Saul's offer, which was to pay them an extreme amount of money to give up the name Creedence Clearwater Revival. They did. John told all of them not to do that because he felt that they could beat him.

Of course, that led to them parting ways. John was so angry that he let them know that he wasn't going to share the stage with them when they were inducted into the Rock and Roll Hall of Fame. It never did get fully reconciled.

I did play on a John Fogerty record about ten years ago, and we were able to talk about that situation. He had come to terms with it. It was so difficult because Saul kept going after him—suing him and suing him. He held off his royalties for all of those great songs because of the copyrights. John had to sue to get them, and he won. The legal issues continued for years. It's finally over. I also saw him last April, and he's in a better place. I can only imagine the stress that comes along with all of that. It definitely took a mental toll on him. It was like torture to the poor guy. He finally got most of that resolved, and he's in a great place.

He's still a great singer and player. He hasn't lost a thing. He doesn't talk about that stuff much anymore.

I saw that Doug and the others have Creedence Clearwater Revival touring again.

That's a lot to deal with.

Yeah, it was a shame to sit there and watch it even from my perspective. I wasn't anybody at the time. It was tough to be privy to all of that: watching one of the biggest groups in the world go through such an ordeal. I was maybe twenty-one years old at the time.

Was that kind of a wake-up call about how the business can be?

Well, preceding all of that, I had seen a lot in New Jersey and Las Vegas. I worked there for a year and a half with the Checkmates as a surrogate, which you probably heard about in the Hall of Fame interview. The musical director, Joe Romano, moved to Oakland and facilitated me moving there. He told me to get an education, and he also had a band out there. I was able to go there and go to Laney College.

I guess you started to think about moving to Nashville about that time.

I knew some people out here. I remember being told that it was one of the last communities—this is around 1973 or 1974—that still had an ensemble in the studio. I wasn't pursuing studio work so much as I was trying to make a living. I wasn't subject to saying, "Oh, man, I want to be a studio player," or anything, for that matter. I had some "secular" jobs, so to speak.

In 1974, I heard that they were looking for a piano player at the Carousel Club [in Nashville]. I got in line with all of the other piano players, auditioned, and ended up getting the gig. Larrie Londin was the drummer. He just came up and said, "I really like you, and you're the guy."

What was the Carousel Club like? Was it a big place?

Not that big. It was a tiered venue that had a downstairs with an upstairs balcony. Jimmy Hyde, who owned it, was a supporter when Boots Randolph came to town. He helped Boots, Chet Atkins. . . . So, I got to know him, and I felt that support too by being in his club. It was pretty much an every-night gig. The money really helped. It gave me confidence in my career to have that steady work. I knew that any work

I could get during the day was extra income that helped me afford to live. It worked out great.

What were some of the other great places to play in Nashville around that time?

There were several. Printer's Alley was a group of venues that was great to play. There was a place called Possum Holler that was George Jones's so-called venue. Club owners would court an artist and give them, say, 10 percent to use their name. That's how that worked. There was a rock club called the Glass Menagerie that I liked. Then there was a place called the Backstage which was a top-forty club. The owner of that had a five-night-a-week situation where his band would play, and he was in the band. Most of the people who wanted that type of music frequented the place every night. It was packed every night.

I'm getting a little ahead of myself. I should say that while I was working with Larrie, he was helping me with playing drums. I told him that he inspired me, and that I really wanted to learn to play. He'd take me upstairs and show me some stuff. When he got into all of the technical stuff, I told him, "I really don't want to know that. I've been trained all my life in the interpretive mode. I just want to beat these things" [laughs].

That's pretty bold to go from being a working pianist and deciding to switch to playing the drums for a living. Was that a difficult transition?

It was what was inside of me. That's what I needed to do, so I did it. There were no barriers that I had to overcome, so to speak. I had the club gig to sustain me and get me through the period to where I could start auditioning for drum gigs. That's what I was about to say earlier, that I auditioned and got the gig playing drums at the Backstage.

And then you were playing drums five nights a week?

Yep. That gave me an opportunity to find even more work. I heard about a studio called Audio Media that was starting in a house over on Division Street. I knew two of the owners. I walked in with Paul Worley, who had just graduated from Vanderbilt with a psychology degree. We both walked in and offered to work for them for free if they would pay us when they had some money. We knew they weren't able to pay us at the time as a start-up. There wasn't really a price on how much we wanted, but we just made it known that they could pay us when they could pay us.

Audio Media and Odyssey Productions were not mainstream businesses. These guys were getting jingles, soundalikes, y'know—out-of-the-box accounts. They were getting work with National Geographic and Disney. So we did that.

Paul and I spent most of our time there probably until 1980. He was already being courted as a producer. We had actually done some of his projects at Audio Media, but then he got to thinking that he would like to have his own facility. At that time, I was very knowledgeable about real estate. I had a building that was over 7,200 square feet. It has 3,600 square feet upstairs and downstairs. So I told him that we could build a studio. We did, and it was called the Money Pit. We spent twenty-seven years being very productive with that facility.

Where was that located?

It's over by the Fairgrounds. I sold it to Dan Rudin, who is a great engineer. Needless to say, I was very pleased to be able to sell something that I felt was a legacy in my life to somebody so worthy. Coincidentally, the studio is still the sort of the same outside-of-the-box place. Dan does orchestral dates simultaneously in New York and Los Angeles over the Internet with ProTools. He's very successful.

What was your drum setup like back then, as opposed to your current setup?

Everything has come full circle. At that time, I was only using acoustic drums, which was great, and no electronics. As I got more involved with studio work outside of Audio Media and doing records, I had to try different things.

I was doing a record for an artist named Deborah Allen. Of course, her husband, Rafe Van Hoy, was producing, and it was engineered by Chuck Ainlay. We tried new ways of doing things. At that point, we had the Simmons SDS-5, not the stereotype sound, but we used the impact of the pads and the noise from the unit to enhance the drums in the mix. We took extra [Shure] 57 microphones and plugged them into the unit and used those to mix. It really did create a great sound.

What happened was, she was on RCA, she turned the record in, and Tony Brown [in A&R] loved it. He played it for Jimmy Bowen, who, yeah, he has a tremendous legacy here. He got infatuated with the sound and was like, "How are you getting this sound?" He wanted that sound on his records.

At that time, Wendel was just starting their little Wendel samples and stuff. [Bowen] was like, "Oh, man, if we could just get that Wendel kick drum onto the real kick drum . . ." At that time, they had this antiquated method called an AMS that could load the sample in and trigger off of the kick. The problem was that, no matter what you did, there was a fifteen-millisecond delay [laughs]. Needless to say, I can't listen to some of those records. It's like, "Man, that feels awful. It *sounds* good, but it feels terrible" [laughs].

And then he went to the next godforsaken thing and got digital drums with the pads and everything. That was an even worse thing. I really can't listen to those records these days. We used them on some records with Reba [McEntire] and George Strait. Man, those drum sounds are terrible [laughs].

When you did use real drums, did you have bottom heads on the drums in that era?

Pretty much, I mostly followed Larrie's lead. We were using, not RotoToms, but Pearl's fiberglass drums. All the toms, other than the floor tom and kick, were totally fiberglass. Then they used fiberwood for the floor tom and kick. They finally realized that wood drums are the best way to go.

I read a Jeff Porcaro interview in which he discussed Steely Dan using the Wendel system, as well as some others. Were all of the popular studios outfitted with a good selection of the different electronic systems at the time?

Well, they were because of the need to be competitive. Sometimes Bowen, having the influence that he did, would set the precedent, which is no different than a studio owner owning something that every-body else buys. The format was a thirty-two-track digital mixing ma-chine. You had to have one to be compatible if you wanted overage and overdub work with everybody else's methods. Then the next thing was a forty-eight-track machine.

You were active during the switch from analog to digital record-ing.

Right.

People always talk about the change in the sound. Did that have an impact on the way you were playing?

It made me more involved electronically. You had to have a refrigerator-sized rack of gear filled with an Akai sampler, ddrum and Simmons modules, and a mixer so that you could trigger your own drums and send the mix to the engineer. That was going on for quite a while.

Was that an exciting time for you?

Well, everything enhances what I was doing. It's great when I could hear the snare sound bigger than it's supposed to be. After a while, you begin to realize what you're hearing isn't reality. Basically samples for me were reverbs. I would use samples that were more enhanced by a reverb versus one that was a true snare drum. It was great because you could do things to your drums.

I imagine that you got a feel for what engineers were looking for with your blend of samples.

Yeah, I had a lot of freedom.

Let's back up for a minute. You mentioned, of course, Larrie Londin being a major influence. You also mentioned in another interview in the *Nashville Scene* that Al Jackson Jr. and Clyde Stubblefield were influences. Can we talk a little more about Larrie and what he meant to you as a drummer?

When you're playing piano, which isn't usually the case, you get to watch him. He would just do things that made me think, "Wow! He's incredible." He was rock solid. He had an incredible foot. He would do things with his foot that would overwhelm you. He had speed and a great placement with his foot. We would come to a breakdown in songs, and it would just be wonderful. Basically, his feel was impeccable.

Larrie was unique because, as a big man, he could be the policeman in a session. If he saw musicians slacking off or talking on the phone too much, he'd stop them. He'd tell them, "We're here to serve these people. Let's work." He was kind of like a fearless leader.

I've heard some rumors about his bass drum pedal.

I've got that story [laughs]! During the year I spent with him, I got good enough to play drums on some things. He was going out with either Chet Atkins or Waylon Jennings pretty frequently. There was one weekend he was going out, and he told Jimmy Hyde, "Look, rather than hire another drummer for the weekend, Eddie knows all of the songs. Let him play drums." And I'm going, "Yeah!" That was a great opportunity.

This was a three-hour gig. I had done gigs of that length before, so that wasn't the problem. I'll never forget sitting down with my foot on his kick pedal. I was trying to push it, and it wouldn't go down. I thought he had locked it because he didn't want anybody to play his drums. So I'm still trying to push it down, I put more weight on it, and it finally went "Boom!" And I thought, "Oh, my God! That's not human." I looked at the pedal, and there was no way to loosen the spring. It was set because it was a custom pedal. There was no way to adjust it. I frantically went up and down [Printer's Alley] trying to find anybody who had an extra pedal that I could use. I found somebody. Yeah, Larrie's pedal was not going to work for me.

Larrie had logs for legs [laughs]. He had the power to be able to use that pedal. But, man, that pedal was scary.

How do you have your pedal set?

It's a pretty medium setting. I play from my toe so I can put some power behind it. I keep it pretty medium.

Are you a lefty naturally?

No, not naturally. I had an accident in 1985 that hurt my left arm. All my normal way of playing went away because I was out of work for eight months. It broke the scaphoid bone, and they had to replace that with a pin and another scaphoid to get the ability to pivot back. I can't bend my left wrist. It's almost like a Les Paul thing where the orthopedic surgeon is asking, "Well, if you do play again, how will you hold the sticks?" And I told him, "Like this" [holds hands openhanded]. And he said, "Okay, but your left hand can't withstand the impact of a snare drum hit again."

The conventional way [right hand over left to play the hi-hat] wasn't going to work because of my injuries. So I spent a lot of desperate time retraining my mind to play openhanded and it stuck. I still switch up at different times because it's a different feel.

I've heard different drummers talk about that, saying they'll open their hands up from time to time to alter the feel of a song.

Yeah, it all depends on what your mind is able to absorb and feel comfortable with. I love to watch Billy Cobham, and he often goes openhanded. It isn't a hindrance to him. It's interesting.

Would you say Larrie Londin, as a player, was very aggressive?

Oh, yeah! The thing about Larrie was that he was a secret weapon. When he would go to specific clinics, there was a stereotype about a drummer from Nashville. He would come in, people would see him, and maybe some of his educational tapes, and think, "Holy smokes!" [laughs]. I mean, he didn't want for anything on the technical side. He knew all that, obviously.

I teach at Berklee College of Music part-time. Part of the premise of my teaching is that we respect that there are clinicians out there that literally go around the drum set, and have the capability to groove. I can say that eight out of ten students are going to be team players rather than solo clinicians for a living. You aren't going to be playing a crazy number of notes to sustain a career as a professional drummer in most cases.

You can aspire to that, but if you want to make a living, like I have, the mind-set is that you first have to wipe the concept of "genre" out of your mind. You can't think that a style of music is greater or lesser because then we're talking about the listeners' preferences, and we're serving them every day. The guy that paves the road, roofs the house, or paints signs is not going to listen to the Mahavishnu Orchestra and get it.

I don't mean that in a demeaning way. In their day-to-day lives of service, the great songwriters write songs that say what the nonsongwriter can't say. In another way, we [drummers] put a beat to songs so the public can go out and dance. So with my students in their formative years at Berklee, I make sure that they wipe out their impression that a style of music is better than another. They are free to work on improving their technique, but they need to understand that they will be a part of a group or production company that is going to deal with all kinds of music.

I also tell my students that they need to understand why Buddy Harman playing "Pretty Woman," "Only the Lonely," or with Patsy Cline is great. I tell them that I can help them there because it's groove. It doesn't matter how simplistic it is—whether it's a brush and a stick, fours on a snare, or something—it has a great feel. And that's something that you *have* to accomplish. If you don't have that, all your technical ability will be meaningless. Productions companies and artists are going to want you to be "meat and potatoes."

You know, you could be in a great jazz-fusion or rock-fusion band, and they break up. The next thing you know, there's a country band that needs a drummer. You don't want to go in thinking that's less valid than the jazz-fusion gig because you need a paycheck.

So you need to find out why all of those songs are great. You need to really take them in, understand them, and appreciate them. Otherwise, you're going to manufacture a performance, and that's very detectable even though it's subliminal. Nearly everybody in that production that has that background will be able to hear it.

Do you hear any of Larrie Londin's influence in your playing?

The main thing is that he was a human quantizer. You aspire to that. I put a lot of effort into being great with a click. It's like this: sometimes a producer comes back to a team and says, "It needs to be a little slower." If I said that to a guitar player and piano player who had a tempo in their head, they would probably pick a new tempo that was ten to fifteen beats slower than where they started.

Being great with a click means that I can pull the tempo back half a beat per minute or one beat per minute, let everybody get that in their head, and then shut it off. As you know, as a percussionist, people, even great musicians, just can't feel one beat per minute slower on their own. They'll be surprised to feel at the end of the intro that it really does feel slower and different.

More relaxed?

Oh, absolutely. So, and now with the technology today, you have to play with a click. In modern production, they wanted the capability to virtually record. So if you run it down once and it's good, but everybody wants to do it again, they can use your take as a template. Everybody will play on top of it. Then the producer can say, "I liked what you did on such-and-such a take," and pull that up. That's called "playlisting." Once they get the nuts and bolts there, they'll start playlisting. Being real consistent gives the engineer more of a capability to use different things because it is consistent on the grid.

The other thing I do well is I can take a band, do four different takes with the same click, and make it sound like four different clicks. Everybody isn't going to be dead on a click. They'll use it as a center—maybe play a verse ahead of the click, pull back for the chorus, or whatever. It's great, I think, that the technology can go further than we can with an artist in the studio.

The artist or producer is going to have to deal with a record label that might say that they want a guitar part louder in a section. In the old days, the engineer would have to pull up that whole mix because he didn't have a snapshot console and try real hard to get it right. SSL created a template where you could log all of that, but it was a painstaking process of turning each knob to the proper place. Now, you can call up the session—it's instantaneous—bump up the guitar, print the mix, and that's it.

That's convenient.

Very, because you never know what you're going to be up against when it comes to the full development of an album. In fact, this just happened. I'm working with this artist called Josh Thompson. We turned the record in, and the guy says, "It needs to be a click faster." And you think, "Well, okay." So you bring it back. I have software called Serato that can click it up one beat per minute, and you won't hear any extra artifacts or degradation.

In this case, I decided not to use it. Instead, I added some shakers and tambourines to it to give them the impression of it being faster. They listened to it and said, "Yeah, that's it." We didn't change it [laughs].

Talking about your influences, like Clyde Stubblefield and Al Jackson Jr., is there anybody else that you felt helped shape your playing?

You know, every time you hear an effort that feels great and has a great consistency, you want to know who it is. Roger Hawkins is one. I got to know him very well. Man, he has a great diversity and ability to groove. He doesn't have to think everything through. It's just part of who he is.

I try to teach that. I tell students, "Look, if I'm just playing a basic groove—a dotted quarter to eighth note followed by a half note thing—we all play that when necessary. I promise you, when you play it, it's going to be you. It will be different than me. There's going to be some minute change in that feel, but it's still going to be great. That's what makes you special. The more freedom you can have playing that groove, the more you are expressing it in a way that is unique to you."

When you think about "Tonight's the Night" with Rod Stewart, "Main Street" with Bob Seger, "Kodachrome" by Paul Simon, or Roger's [Hawkins] work with Aretha Franklin, the Staple Singers . . . those are all great records! They still feel good today.

I also love Mitch Mitchell. I knew Mitch really well all the way up to his last days. *He* was reckless abandon on the drums for me. Anybody that could do all of that—I mean, if any of us *tried* to do that . . .

Get away with it?

You couldn't [laughs]. It wouldn't be natural to have that fire, almost like playing a solo in a song. It was unique. That was his expression. It was freeing to me to hear that. I wouldn't try to duplicate that. I was inspired by who he was, what he did, and his style of playing.

Buddy Harman, to me, was the second person that I really studied. Larrie was the inspiration, but Buddy was really the art. He was ahead of his time. He played all those grooves on all those great records. You could hear sounds of different things and wonder what it was. He'd say, "That was a tape box that I played on." And I'm thinking, "Tape box? Really?" Or he told me that he was playing on a guitar body for a song to get different sounds. I said, "I'll bet whenever you mention trying something like that a bunch of Martins [high-quality acoustic guitars] get in the cases before you finish the sentence" [laughs].

That's really interesting. So how often do you get an opportunity to experiment with different ideas like that?

Oh, I do! I've done some unique things even with electronics, when I was using them, that still sound good a decade later. It's kind of like stepping outside of yourself, listening, and wondering, "How'd I do that?" There was spontaneity to those moments. I remember a Kris McKay song called "Could Talking Be Like Dancing." I had my rims set to a sample of backward cymbals. The floor tom was set to an explosion. I played a conga pattern on the snare drum with sticks. The kick drum and cross stick were normal. The total effort ended up being pretty incredible.

Early on in my session career, I started experimenting with the hand-on-snare-drum stuff—playing different patterns on an open snare. I did that on some of the earlier records. I played the back of a guitar as a backbeat on the Judds's "Why Not Me?"

As much as I could take that influence to get out of the norm, even though the norm would have been perfectly fine, I would do things to be unique. Sometimes it's as simple as keeping the snares off for the verse, and turning them on for the chorus. Those types of things really create a nice diversity.

That's about as far as you can go. There are only so many things you can do with an acoustic set to change it up. I've used boxes. I did a record with Rodney Crowell. We recorded it all in a circle. It's not out yet. He actually made me a box to play on the record. Even better than that, he has a book out about his life and experiences [*Chinaberry Sidewalks*]. He said, "I just want to tell you that I put all of my rough drafts of the book inside this box for you." So it's like a time capsule.

What is your process for selecting your drums?

One of the greatest things I got to do was go to Japan to visit the Yamaha facility when I signed with them. They gave me an opportunity to personally oversee the putting together of my drum set. It was really interesting because they had this big schematic on a board before you even go into the manufacturing facility. You can see everything drawn out. They show you that a beveled edge does certain things sonically, and they talked me through a bunch of information. I said, "You know what [laughs]? I don't build drums. I don't know anything about that. I just know what sounds good. You guys build more that drums. You've got great pianos, guitars, and basses. So I'll yield to you on these decisions because you understand how things translate sonically through wood better than I do. So what do you recommend?"

Very interestingly, they said, "One simple thing is that when you see a solid wrap, that's a film that compresses the drum. It might sound good to you, but not necessarily to an engineer that knows what he's doing because it will take more work to get a great tone. We recommend just wood." So I said, "Okay."

I've always been a fan of birch toms and a maple kick. A birch kick never worked for me. That's my kit. It was neat to watch them pick the wood and then form it into a shell. A twelve-inch tom starts out about three feet long, and then they ask you which part of the grain you want. That was fun to pick. Then they cut, sand, and ask what kind of finish. I got to pick the vintage black.

I made that trip around 2005.

What gear were you using when you first started playing drums?

I played some Pearl drums and even had a Remo drum set. I was signed to Remo when they started making drums. The problem was that they were doing the same thing as Pearl and not making wood drums. I kept telling them that a lot of the engineers that I'm working with really want wood drums. They just told me, "Well, we just don't make them." That led me to sign with Pearl, and I was with them for thirteen years. They had started making wood drums by then. They were great drums, and then I went to Yamaha.

We've been talking about sounds. It got me thinking about how every room you work in has a particular sound. Going back to Audio Media, was that an acoustically good room to work in?

As much as we knew, it was good. It certainly wasn't what we would call state-of-the-art. For the time, it served its purpose. We did a lot of stuff at that studio. It was a real good training ground for Paul [Worley] to become the great producer that he is today.

He and I were multipurpose there. We would play on records and then spend the rest of the night singing background vocals. We put enough of a leader on the analog tape so that we could run out into the room in time for the vocal parts. When we got to a place where we could actually hire background vocalists, we got to record them. I think that really added to Paul's talent as a producer to be able to orchestrate vocals as he's done. His latest is Lady Antebellum and, as you know, he makes great records.

Were there other studios in town at the time that you thought sounded good and loved to work in?

That's an interesting question. There's no way to explain why you can walk in one room and, no matter what you do, you just don't feel that it works—the vibe or whatever. You can be in a three-million-dollar facility and it just doesn't feel right. But you can go into a room like this [the Rukkus Room] or maybe some brand new place, and it just feels great.

There were so many places that we were working. Unfortunately, a lot of them are gone due to the downturn in the music industry. There has also been a rise in the number of home studios and producers' home studios—which are really office studios—and that's changed how things are done. People know that they can go to a big room, cut their tracks, and then take them home to finish them. It's difficult for the big facilities to survive.

I remember sitting in a friend's place working on some demos. He had a pretty state-of-the-art studio in his house. He's a virtuoso and plays every instrument. So I had him play bass, guitar, mandolin, and whatever. I said, "Man, did you hear about Emerald Sound? We cut so many great records there. Did you hear they filed for bankruptcy?" And he said, "Man, what happened?" I turned, pointed at his setup, and said, "Look at that!" He replied, "Oh, right" [laughs].

So I'm finding that the studios that are surviving, and there are studios that are doing well, are the places that are owned by people with deep pockets that really want a studio. The guy that owns Black River Music, which was Ronnie Milsap's studio, just bought SoundStage next door. He's gone in and redone it. It's a great state-of-the-art room. He's a billionaire.

Then you've got Reba [McEntire] and StarStruck. It's a great, great studio. The Tracking Room is owned by Dale Morris, who has been a very successful manager for years. He's managed Kenny Chesney and Alabama, so he has the ability to keep that facility going. Actually, it wasn't a studio when he bought it. A guy came in who was the head of Masterfonics originally and converted it into a studio. We always thought it was strange to put three million dollars into something you didn't own. I guess he had a long enough leash that he felt comfortable.

Of course, John McBride owns Blackbird Studios, and that's facilitated between his success and Martina's. He built what is probably the largest facility, with so many rooms delegated for different things. He had the attitude to say, "To bring engineers, I'll give them a room to do their work." George Massenburg moved out, but Dann Huff and Paul Worley use that room.

Again, those studios don't survive by waiting for the phone to ring. They have the ability to withstand the lows in the industry. With my studio, it was easy because I had one of the most popular producers in Nashville. Paul kept that place going.

You know, RCA Room B is a tourist attraction now, although they will use it for special recording projects. I did an Elvis record there about four years ago. They opened the studio and we played to Elvis's voice. We had a tempo map. That's historical to get in. In more cases than not, it would have to be something of merit like that. Otherwise, you'll see Studio B on the tour. You can go through and see all of the original equipment.

There's a lot of history in RCA Room B. Have you ever been in a room where you felt proud to be in a place where so much great music had been recorded?

Having Elvis on my discography was cool. It was exciting going into that session knowing that Elvis had worked there. That was a special thing to be in that place and take it all in.

That's interesting. I never really felt inspired by a place. To me it was always just another room that had my drums in it with microphones all over the place. It really meant more to other people that weren't connected to it than to us. If I said I just recorded something for Elvis at Studio B, people say, "Oh, wow! That's incredible!" I guess I treasure that time, but we're not exactly overwhelmed. I'm also happy that people have the satisfaction of hearing that stuff. We're used to being in a state-of-the-art room and hearing what comes back.

Again, that's subject to the engineer. Obviously, I'm using great drums and some days they just sound great. Other days, in a different room with a different engineer, I play them, and, yeah, it's pretty uninspiring. Then I'll listen to the playback and think about how good they sounded the day before when they were soaring.

Sometimes I think the era in which a person learned recording plays a large part in their sound. One of the times I was teaching up at Berklee, the professor and I got into a discussion about our favorite recording format. I said that I think that at some point during the process you have to fold into analog. I'm a fan of analog consoles. I know that plug-ins are being made more available that have an analog sound, but there still isn't a replacement for an analog console. The professor made sure to note, "We want to make sure that they can do great things 'in the box.'" I said, "I understand, but as long as we're dealing with state-of-the-art recording, we will have analog consoles."

I've worked in other facilities that are totally digital, and they never sound as good. Even some of the greater digital consoles just don't have it. I don't know what it is—maybe it's bandwidth or EQ—I don't know. Even if a studio is going to be all digital, it still takes an engineer that has dealt with analog to translate what happens in ProTools, Nuendo, or any of the others into what you want people to hear.

You still have to have the knowledge to make that work with what your ear is trained to hear. Those people that have that knowledge are capable of working in either format. Chuck Ainlay remixed [Dire Straits'] "Brothers in Arms" in digital and it sounds great. A lot of schools aren't really teaching those techniques because they don't believe students need that.

That could also be a budget issue at some schools.

Yeah, digital is a lot cheaper and more simple. To me, it would be a worthy investment to use tape. Now they're talking about increasing the sample rate. The technology exists to store a lot of files that are that large. I think iTunes is going through a transition of increasing the quality of their offerings.

I know there is a group called HDtracks where you can get high-quality downloads of great records. An example would be a Paul Simon record. You can get it on iTunes for ten dollars in the Apple loss format, or you can buy it from HDtracks for ten dollars more. The HDtracks version sounds a lot better. That gets into a whole other thing because I don't know if that many people are concerned about hearing music sound that good.

Yeah, kids are listening to music using ear buds.

And MP3s on iPods [laughs]. They exercise with it, work with it, go to sleep with it. They aren't really sitting in front of a 5.1 system taking it all in.

At the end of the day, though, one thing has never changed. When I was growing up, there was a forty-five-minute vinyl record or cassette. Obviously, we can listen to them now and think, "Wow." The bottom line is that those records are great because of the reasons that records are great—a great artist, a great song, and a great feel. People hear that through everything else.

I could take a bad song and put it on the highest-quality media, or I could take a great song and put it on a lower-quality media: people are going to pick the great song. That's the key.

The outside perception of you is that you work with a group of guys very consistently, like with the Players. Is the bulk of your work with that core?

No. We don't see each other very often. I probably see Paul Franklin, Brent Mason, and John Hobbs most frequently from that group.

There are just different production camps. Back in the day when every-thing was a windfall and we were booked seven months in advance, it would depend on who the production camp was going to use.

The thing that I found—let's say you and I found an artist that we really believed in, we would book whoever was available at the time to record the record. To me, the playing field is level now. There are a lot of great musicians. So you and I, record the record, end up getting a deal. Well who are we going to finish the record with? That creates a whole other chemistry.

How long have you known Paul Franklin?

We go back probably to the 1980s.

What were those early sessions like with him? Did you really lock in with him?

You know, I could take the group of people that I mentioned and replace them with other people and it will still be great. I know that they all have specialties, but there are a lot of similarities between players. We are starting to find—I mean me, Paul, Brent, John, and Michael—that there are people that we have inspired over the years, and they always say it. They'll come up and say, "I've listened to you for years and you're such an inspiration." Those players have studied, lis-tened, and they do well.

So there isn't a point where you can listen in your headphones and think, "That's Paul Franklin"?

There's another guy that can dupe me. I would think it was Paul. Paul and Dan Dugmore are steel players but can also take a lap steel and just rock. Of course, Paul's history with Dire Straits helps. Dug-more goes across the board because of his work in Los Angeles and all of those great rock records he played on like "Blue Bayou" with Linda Ronstadt, or his work with James Taylor. You'd have to look at his discography to see his depth. They do have specialties that make you realize they are more than just steel players.

Their choice of fills and licks are great, but they can play things from a different era if a producer asks for it because they know how to do that. Of course, they can let loose if needed.

What are your thoughts on Brent Mason?

I think his diversity makes him real special. He was George Benson's protégé, so he brings that in. He is also able to do that up-tempo picking thing. Once you hear him and watch him, he's like a freak.

Do you guys get a lot of freedom in sessions?

I always compare a great producer to a coach. He isn't going to throw the ball, catch it, and run with it. He brings to the table an inspiration. He isn't going to tell the players how to do what they know how to do. He might suggest different directions for each player to take, but it still comes down to each individual. We all have valid input to be able to give him. We just try to give a lot of choices.

If you had us in a session, it's automatic. Somebody will start suggesting that maybe the intro can be cut in half, or fold in the instrumental in the last bar instead of a setup, or perhaps some major editing. I see it all the time.

Who are your favorite bass players to work with?

Michael Rhodes is right up there. I met him in 1977. I work with Glenn Worf a lot and Mike Brignardello. I like Kevin Grant. There's a new kid named Eli Beard, who is the son of Larry Beard of Beard Music Group, and I love his playing. You can hear all the inspiration of his playing.

What was your first meeting with Michael Rhodes like?

We were both brought in. I had already been at Sony for around two years. That was more of a demo house with some great writers. They hired him. He and I just connected at that point. He brought me into the Rodney Crowell/Roseanne Cash gig because he was working with Rodney. We looked after each other for many years.

Did you form the Players?

Yep.

What was your inspiration for starting that?

I was always into the so-called politics around here. I became a member of the board of governors for NARAS a long time ago and did that for eighteen years. I met a lot of people through that. I was also the first graduate of Leadership Music and met a lot of people there. The one benefit from that is you are in there with the top of the food chain. The one thing that our facilitator told us was that there were thirty-five of us and we will all answer each other's calls when needed.

Martin Clayton, the head of CMT.com, was a part of that. I met with him and told him that I had some ideas. One of them was doing a Christmas special with Brenda Lee. She decided not to do it, so I used Glen Campbell. After that, I wanted to create a show using great musicians that I worked with paired with renowned artist-musicians. He thought it was a great idea and told me to get my band together. That's when I handpicked the members of the Players. That was around ten years ago.

You guys have a regular gig downtown.

Not *too* regular because we work so much, but we're playing tomorrow night at 3rd & Lindsley. It's usually whenever we can. We're certainly not doing it for a living. That group has just stuck together. I don't know if you saw excerpts from the DVD, but I brought in Peter Frampton, Michael brought in Shawn Colvin, John brought in Vince Gill. We all brought in Alan Jackson and Jim Horn, whom we all love. Travis Tritt worked with us too. It was a great show. From that, the Players were born. We just said, "Okay, this is going to be a band."

3rd & Lindsley is like Nashville's Baked Potato.

It is. There is a diversity there of every kind of music you would ever want to hear. We're a pretty eclectic group. We do revisit a couple of old songs by people like Lou Rawls, but we do commercial jazz. That's us, but you can go and see the Wooten Brothers. Pat McLaughlin has a band.

Ron [Brice] has done such a great thing with that club. It's very comfortable since it has expanded. The renovations are phenomenal. They still need to tweak the sound a little. We were there last week. You could see where it was different from the old hole in the wall—which *was* really good. Now, it's more of a state-of-the-art room.

You're also in a band called the Notorious Cherry Bombs. How did that come about?

That actually came from Larrie. When Rodney [Crowell] started the Cherry Bombs years ago, Larrie was the drummer. Vince [Gill] was the guitar player, and Hank DeVito played steel guitar. They were a pretty well-known group because they worked with Emmylou Harris, Roseanne Cash, and some others.

Rodney started the group. When it came time to do a reunion, maybe around 2008, they picked me because of Larrie. It was interesting. We had a major record deal. Of course, Rodney and Vince wrote everything. We just went in and did the project. Of course, that wasn't going to stick because Vince's management felt it took away from his solo career. Vince has enough power to do whatever he wants at this point.

Vince Gill seems like one of those artists that has real street cred among the great players.

He is very focused. He is a *great* guitar player, and his vocals are through the roof. We know that in this day and age we can make an average singer sound great with vocal fixing technology. He's one that doesn't need any help. He sings the song once, maybe fixes a word, and that's the vocal take.

What is the Medallion Band?

That started several years back. There was always a band that hosted the inductees of the Country Music Hall of Fame. The premise is that the inductees are allowed to choose who they want to perform a tribute to them in song. We were the backing band for those selected artists. We just did it in May and do it every year. It's a specialty group. We know going in that we are going to get to work with legends and do great songs.

Who is in the group?

The core is the Players. We then augment the core with whatever is needed—a fiddle, mandolin, acoustic guitar, or whatever. A lot of times that changes according to availability. It can also change according to who we're backing up.

Hobbs is basically the musical director. That's been going on for about five years. There was a different band before us. For whatever reason, they decided to change the group.

You did bring up your role with NARAS. What do you do with them?

They of course facilitate the Grammys. They do more than that. I've always been interested in groups like NARAS, CMA, or the Academy of Country Music that go beyond their television productions with philanthropic endeavors.

I know that NARAS has MusiCares and Grammy in the Schools.

Oh, MusiCares is one of the biggest. They also do a lot of education-al things with, say, Jimmy Jam, who is a great supporter. He's on the board too. They pick the board of governors from that group. They meet once a month and address specific delegations like education, events, and other facets that they participate in through their founda-tion. It's very important to be able to recruit and find those people that don't realize they are qualified to vote. You have to have been involved in the creative aspect of a top-ten record.

I just decided it was time for some new blood after the sixteen or eighteen years that I was involved. After a while, you know the protocol and there's a lot of time involved. It isn't just that there's a meeting once a month, but there are events that you are involved with. It takes a lot of time. It's definitely worthwhile, but sometimes your time runs out. I did my part.

I did a lot for Grammy in the Schools and in the colleges. I put together panels. It was kind of like what I do at Berklee with Roger Brown in March. Every year for a week, they bring around 120 students down to Nashville, and we program different topics that we can discuss. I've even used lessons that I learned from Leadership Music as part of the curriculum.

This past March I had Bob Doyle, who managed Garth Brooks. I brought in the head of A&R for Curb Records, Doug Johnson. I had Steve Buckingham, who not only ran Sony but also ran Vanguard Records. So we created panels, and the students were able to have one-on-one stuff. They got information that they never would have been able to get. We also set up some artist one-on-ones. I brought in Alison Krauss, Vince Gill, Rodney Crowell, and Delbert McClinton.

We always end the week with a recording session. Obviously, you need a large recording facility to accommodate 120 students. We used the Tracking Room. We do a 2 p.m. to 5 p.m. session. We have an artist come in. This year we had Vince Gill as the artist. He is very informa-tive. He is able to relate who he is and what he's doing in a song. We'll write a chart as he's playing it. He'll say something about the song, we'll talk about the chart, and then we go in and record it. The song is finished at the end of the session. The students get to see all of that. In a sense, NARAS does the same thing in a whole different way with schools and colleges. When I did events for NARAS, we did it in pretty much the same format.

Do you have any favorite songs or records that you have played on?

That's a tough one. Most of the songs that I've done were maiden voyages for the artists that became great artists. With Vince, it was "When I Call Your Name." The Judds, obviously, "Why Not Me?" and "Mama He's Crazy." Alan Jackson "Chasin' That Neon Rainbow." On the other side, I did three albums with Bob Seger. In fact, he's recording a new album now. I did three sides on his last album. I did a side on Steve Winwood's record.

As you can imagine, there are efforts that I did that you haven't heard. They were on major labels, but nothing ever happened. Yeah, there are songs on some records that I think, "Man! That represents me," but they're so outside that they don't get released.

You just reminded me of something I saw when I was doing research for this interview. You did some work with Sting, but I can't seem to find any recordings from that.

That came from a duet record and even included Elton John. Tammy Wynette had an idea about doing a duets project, and these great artists that respected Tammy came through. We went to Atlanta and recorded with Elton John. He's a sweetheart. He had an attitude of, "Tell me what you want." He was there to serve.

The beauty of Sting was that we did "Every Breath You Take," and he played bass on it. I was thinking, "Oh, man! I can't believe this! I'm playing this with him!" We became, at least, acquaintances through that. I worked with him a couple of other times like on the CMA awards and stuff like that. He's very likable.

He had great respect for all of us. He has great musicianship. He and Elton never brought in an ego. You don't feel any of that other stuff.

What do you think are the critical musical attributes somebody should have to be successful?

Well, I can utilize the template that I use at Berklee. The first thing I do is take a poll. I say, "Obviously, we're all musicians here. We're creative. We have something inside of us that tells us what we think is great or bad, what's complex or easy." I've made a great living for forty-five years. I've secured my assets; my family is taken care of. Everybody's doing well. I don't like to flaunt the fiscal stuff, but what else are you trying to do? Obviously, we want to make a statement as musicians, but we also need to remember that there isn't much better than making a living doing it.

Now we're talking about what I want to convey, and that is that you need to wipe out genre. There's no genre. There are great artists. I hear people say things like, "I don't like country music, but I love Keith Urban." I want to ask them if they have been listening to country music lately. There's Keith Urban and Taylor Swift. Then you look at some of their predecessors like Martina McBride. They still come under "country." People need to understand that genre is more than style.

The true hard lines of genre were created by corporations. Sony has divisions like Pop, Classical, and Country. All of that is so that the people that facilitate these releases get money in their can. That's basically it. The pie is what delegates divisions. I submit to you that any great artist—like Mark Knopfler and his *Golden Heart* record, for example—you'll hear who he is and you'll only hear two country songs. We used Pig Robbins for keyboards.

You'll see that even Sting used Paul Franklin on *Ten Summoner's Tales*. These people don't have any barriers. They aren't going to say that they're rock musicians and not using anybody else. People can't survive like that unless they're part of some famous group. Yeah, those guys can do what they want. The reality is that people that have longevity will learn to disregard those divisions.

Don't think that just because you have heard the greatest clinician in the world that there's some difference between him or her as compared to the "meat and potatoes" guy. Most of the guys that I introduce you to—Steve Gadd or others—I can take you back to examples of him playing for Frank Sinatra and kicking a big band like you've never heard before. Then you hear "50 Ways to Leave Your Lover." Then you meet him and realize that he speaks the same musical language. Dave Weckl is a good friend of mine. It's the same thing. I witness it all the time.

I judge the Drum Off for Guitar Center. I hear these wizards come in. It's really funny because they know that I'm on the panel, so they think that they have to put a groove in their solo. They're thinking, "Man, I have to put a groove in here because he's thinking I'm not going to be able to do all of this stuff on my next session." It's funny how they sometimes break off into a groove and it doesn't groove.

If there's any advice I give them, it's that. I tell them that they've definitely crafted all of their stuff, but they really need to figure out why something grooves. They're manufacturing a groove and not really performing it. It's interesting. Of course, that isn't everybody. Some of those guys come in and have such a great ebb and flow and can do it all. All of their technical stuff grooves too. There's something about the beginning to end of their solos that just works from beginning to end. That's what I mostly want to convey.

I sometimes even get more hard-core and ask, "How many want to make a living like I've done for forty-five years and know that you've secured yourself?" Of course they all raise their hands. So I'll say, "Well, don't misunderstand this, but Ringo Starr is the richest drummer in the world." They're thinking, "What!?!"

I imagine Charlie Watts is right up there with him.

Yeah. You know, when you look at it, I'm just trying to tell them that the best thing a person can do is keep their judgment to themselves. For every great record, there are a million people who love it and a million who don't. What matters is the million who love it. Everybody else is going to be just fine making their residuals and getting ready to do another one. You can hate it all you want, but it pays the bills.

I'm sure you've seen it. There are so many things that people just immediately blurt out of their mouth. I met Kenny G's drummer the other day. He and I got to talking, and I said, "Kenny G takes such a hit on everything he does. For some reason, people just stereotype the guy." He's sold millions of records, you buy his coffee everyday—you know he's one of the founders of Starbucks.

The point is, you've got to understand what you're doing when you open your mouth about things. You could get up there and I could put you in that same seat. If I put a panel in here, would you want to hear what they had to say? Would you want to hear somebody say, "Aw man, you suck!" or "You don't play like some other guy"?

That's an unfortunate reality of the Internet.

That stuff happens. Some DJ's came through town to record a session. It was with Steve Wariner. They put the video up without the music and it's just me playing a shuffle. There were some nice comments, but this one guy wrote, "You couldn't swing if you hung him."

Then I'd started looking at the comments. I even saw Leland Sklar writing responses to that nonsense asking who that guy thought he was.

The problem is people seem to have forgotten that old saying that goes something like, "It's better to keep your mouth shut and be thought a fool, then to open it and remove all doubt." I've always thought that people need to keep a clear, open mind about everything. Your opinions are just opinions. Years ago, I started my own magazine because I wanted to give artists the last word.

I was interviewed a few years ago by *MusicRow* magazine. This girl started talking about me, and she said, "You also produce, right?" I said, "Minimally. I coproduced a record with Roseanne Cash called *Interiors* and also the Players. We were all coproducers on the Cherry Bombs album." She asked if she could get copies of those so she could review them. I told her, "You can either shut off the recorder now, or record what I'm going to tell you."

So I said, "What gives you the power to review those records?" She replied, "David Ross—he's the head of the magazine—said I could review records." So I asked, "What's the last hit song you wrote?" She said that she wasn't a songwriter. So I asked, "What's the last hit record you played on?" She said that she didn't have any. So I asked, "If I gave you a chart, would you be able to translate it with any instrument?" She said no. I just kept on going. I asked her if she saw where I was going with my line of questioning.

I told her that I'm sure she did well as a journalism major and that she would be better served getting a job at a newspaper or writing a book. I said, "But don't critique music because, even if you could do those things that I asked you about, it is just your opinion. Those records are successful efforts." My issue with her is that she could say something in that magazine that could hurt somebody. It might stifle their creativity. They might be soft-shelled and sensitive. If she stifles their creativity to further themselves, then I hold her responsible. I asked her, "Is that what you want?" She literally started crying.

I said, "I'm sorry. One thing you see in sports, if you look at the people in the commentary booth, most of them played the game—especially now." It used to be that there were TV personalities like Howard Cosell, but now you're seeing retired quarterbacks holding the microphone. It's important because when they talk about the game, they really know what's happening on the field. They lived it.

As far as I'm concerned, people should have a biography in music before they have the right to say something about it. Even then, they don't have a right. If you can't say something nice, don't say it. Our society will say such hateful things. It's just sad.

And you know what? I'll be the first one to say something back. If somebody starts talking poorly about Kenny G, or even the movie *Ghost*—that movie made millions of dollars, but was widely criticized. I'm thinking, "There's millions of dollars here. There are no millions in your comments. What does that say about you?" It's just an opinion, and that person is a knucklehead [laughs].

As you know, I'm interviewing some other drummers for this book—Kenny Malone, Jerry Kroon, Tommy Wells, and Tom Roady.

Perfect.

Do you have any words to say about them?

They're all brothers. They are all close. I know them all. I respect them all.

When I was signed to Acuff-Rose, I hired Kenny to play on my demos. I was writing songs, so I was there to watch it through.

I didn't know you were signed to Acuff-Rose as a songwriter. When was that?

That was around 1975 or 1976.

Did that last for a while?

I got to a point where I just loved playing more than crafting songs. I wrote an R&B song that the Temptations recorded. I had success as a writer. I just couldn't see myself living like, "Hey Tony, get out your book. Let's write on Tuesday." That's what you have to do. My time isn't going to be taken up by that. That isn't what I felt I was here to do.

I like composing. I'll sit back and write. I have a song on Billy Joe Walker's record. John Jarvis used one of my instrumental songs.

What is your impression of Jerry Kroon?

Jerry's great. Years ago, we were in that group that worked all the time. There's a new group now that I'm working with. We shared records together like Ricky Skaggs. I always listened to what he was doing. He's a great guy and great player.

All these people that you're talking about are people who understood who they were as individuals, and that comes out in their playing.

Tom Roady is such a sweetheart. We have shared a lot of great times in the studio. We worked together on what I consider some of the best records I ever played on. The Suzy Bogguss stuff is excellent. That also had Leland Sklar playing bass. Tom and I were in James Taylor's acoustic band together and did a tour. It was great.

I respect all of these guys highly. They really exemplify what I said earlier about people playing the same thing in different ways. If I were to notate out a groove, each of them would bring their talent and it would be them. All of them are still great.

You can go back for years, and all of them are still here and successful. That says a lot about them. That, to me, is a statement.

Thank you so much.

Man, my pleasure. Let me know if there is anything I can do to help when you're finished.

2

JERRY KROON

Unlike many professional musicians who start playing an instrument at an early age, Jerry Kroon started playing the drums when he was around fifteen years old in South Dakota. Somewhat impressively, he was playing his first gigs before he graduated from high school. After graduation, he began playing with groups that toured regionally before landing a gig with the Velaires, of "Roll Over Beethoven" fame.

After moving to Nashville, Kroon sought out employment as a drummer. It was after he got his first experience in a Nashville recording studio that his desire to record full-time was born. In the meantime, he stayed very busy touring with different artists and performing around Nashville as his recording work became steadier. At the time, it was difficult for touring musicians to secure steady session work. Kroon took a leap of faith after being called for several high-profile recording sessions and made the decision to stop touring in 1979. It turned out to be a wise decision.

Kroon made his mark recording on a high number of country and gospel albums for over two decades. His work with the likes of Ray Stevens, George Strait, Reba McEntire, Willie Nelson, Sawyer Brown, Bill Gaither, and Sammy Kershaw is highly regarded for his ability to create the right groove for the song. He has a keen sensitivity for musical direction and is eager to go the extra mile to make sure everything he works on is completed at the highest level possible. His incredible recording career was recognized with a Lifetime Achievement Award from the South Dakota Rock and Roll Hall of Fame. In this interview, Kroon shows how a patient, humble approach to networking, complemented by a structured approach to practicing the instrument for improvement, can build and sustain a rich musical career.

Let's start with some background information.

I'm from the Midwest. I grew up in a town just outside of Sioux Falls, South Dakota. I started playing professionally my senior year in high school. Unlike a lot of musicians that started at a real early age, I guess I started noodling around when I was fourteen or fifteen. I was always active in sports—basketball and baseball. When I started playing [drums], I was making money by my senior year playing on weekends instead of sacking groceries for fifteen dollars a night [laughs]. I was playing with a piano player making thirty dollars a night. That was probably when I knew that I wanted to do it professionally. I just wanted it really bad. I wanted to make a living playing drums.

The key influence I had was my parents. My mom and dad were always supportive of me. They never said I needed to go to college or anything. I always want to give them credit. They've both passed away now. I'll never forget one of the greatest pieces of advice my dad gave me: if you have passion for something, you'll make a good living and you'll enjoy your life. He said that's the greatest thing you can have: passion for what you do. He worked for a power company, and he loved it. It was outdoors, and he was a foreman. It just always stuck with me. I did have the passion. I don't think I necessarily had the talent that other people had.

South Dakota was my musical root. Right after high school, I got a chance to play with a band called Myron Lee and the Caddies. Back in the late fifties and early sixties, they did all these Dick Clark "Shower of Stars" tours that had one house band that did that. They were very well known. They weren't touring like that when I came into the band, but we were working three or four nights a week doing ballrooms. They had some of the best drummers around.

South Dakota is not like coming to Nashville, where you have five hundred drummers that are really good. South Dakota is limited in population and musicians, but the ones that are there are really good. Bobby Keys played in that band, and he went on to play with the Rolling Stones. Stu Perry was the drummer in the band, and he went on to play with Delaney and Bonnie Bramlett. So there were a lot of people who were quite good and went on to make a good living.

Myron's band was my first really professional gig. This guy made a living, raised his family, bought property, and did all of that doing nothing but playing music. I was with him for a couple of years, and that was a big key for my career.

When you were in high school, you said you were in a piano band. What was that like?

We were playing everything—top-forty stuff, Beatles, a lot of the English stuff, R&B. It was very cool.

So did that teach you a lot about those styles?

Yeah. I was always in club bands. I guess we were a cover band. You would learn the top ten or fifteen songs that were out, and always had

"Johnny B. Goode" on standby. It was a great experience. In fact, it's a big honor to me—South Dakota started a Rock and Roll Hall of Fame three or four years ago. . . . You know, when you go away, you forget about a lot of things that happened twenty or thirty years ago because you're just trying to survive. So they started this Rock and Roll Hall of Fame that was all about the people that had influence on the music around there. What you have to realize is, where I grew up, you could be working three or four nights a week making a full-time living by playing ballrooms, clubs, and other places.

During the week, we played a club called Shorty's, then hit the road Friday through Sunday. There were a lot of very influential bands that were regional stars and had local records and a tremendous following. So the Rock and Roll Hall of Fame has been incredible. There's been like fifteen hundred people paying four hundred to five hundred dollars for tables to see these bands that were popular in Minnesota, Iowa, Nebraska, and Kansas. My wife and I got inducted into that last year [2010]. I got in there with a Lifetime Achievement Award based on what I've done in music. It's a tremendous honor to be recognized by the people that helped get you started. That was a pretty neat deal.

What kind of drums did you have back then?

I had a Rogers kit. I'm not really that hip on gear. Drums are round and I hit them [laughs]. I had pre-CBS Rogers. The first set that I bought was kind of a Joe Morello Ludwig kit. My dad took me to the credit union, and I took out a loan. My payment was thirty-five dollars a month for, I don't know, a year or something. I kept those drums for a while before I got a Rogers set. I think I got a little Gretsch set. I came to Nashville with a Rogers kit and a couple of snare drums.

Back in the Midwest, how did you get your name established?

First of all, you start a local band in your town. You go out and book a gig and hopefully get another gig. Other bands that are higher up in the food chain may take notice, may want to hire you. So experience, word-of-mouth . . . The key thing was getting into bands that worked steady. I was fortunate, and I worked in a lot of bands that worked five or six nights a week. Club bands. It was great.

The biggest disappointment I had back then was during my senior year. I was working with a college band called the Continentals. They had this wonderful opportunity to go to Minneapolis, which, back then, was like working in Las Vegas. It was a place where people longed to work, kind of a like a silver circuit deal where you could make a lot of money. We're talking around 1964, and there were a lot of great places to play. I couldn't go because I was only seventeen, and my dad was not going to let me quit school. I didn't want to quit school either. I got let go because I couldn't do the gig. Those guys were making between four hundred and five hundred dollars a week, which was huge money back then. You could buy a nice house for two hundred dollars a month and get any car you wanted for one hundred or one twenty a month. It was a big blow to me. I was really crushed by that. I thought, "Aww man, this is the end of it for me." I wanted it so bad, but obviously things worked out.

Then I hooked up with Myron. From there, I went to Sioux City and played with the Velaires. It just started going from there. That's when we made the decision to move to Nashville in 1971. My wife and I were working in a club band. She sang, Danny Matousek was the leader who played bass along with his wife, Carolyn. We also had a guitar player and sax player. It was a really great gig, and we had a great life.

We were making double income, bought our first little house in Sioux City, Iowa. Everything was going really great, and then the club where we were working decided to go in a different direction. Something happened. I don't know. I just told my wife, "We need to go to Nashville. We need to get out of here. If we stay, I don't think we'll ever leave. I don't know what's going to happen, but I want to play full-time. I really have to go where there's work." I didn't come here [Nashville] to be a session player. I came here because my common sense told me that there was more opportunity to work in Nashville, possibly on the road with a *Grand Ole Opry* star, than there was in Sioux City, Iowa, with a band that would probably get another club gig. I thought, "What will I do when I'm fifty years old? What kind of opportunity will I have had?"

Let me back up a little bit. In 1969, I had an opportunity to move to Nashville and I took it. I got a call from a friend I met in Sioux Falls when he was off touring. We played one of the country clubs up there—you know, a country and western club. I indicated that I would love to go to Nashville. He called out of the blue and said that Charlie Louvin was looking for a drummer and asked if I would go out with him.

I wasn't married, so I took the opportunity. It was a great opportunity, but it didn't work out. Things were not explained to me financially. I'd left a steady job, and then I was on a floating pay scale where I only got paid when we worked. I was told it paid a hundred and fifty dollars a week. It was fifty dollars less than I was making, but it was okay because I was in Nashville. Well, it was a hundred and fifty a week until winter came about two or three weeks later. Then it dropped down to two days a week, and I learned that it really paid fifty dollars a day. That's when I found out that my idea of a hundred and fifty a week was not the same as everybody else's idea of a hundred and fifty a week [laughs].

Long story made short, I ended up living in a boarding house for about six weeks. I was living with a buddy and had to move out because it wasn't in town. I felt that was important. I made twelve fifty a week working the *Grand Ole Opry* with Charlie Louvin. It wasn't good. I went home, called my fiancée, and said I was coming back to Sioux City.

We got married in December 1970 and moved down here a year later. It's been great ever since—wonderful.

You said that you were playing a lot of top-forty music, like the Beatles. Were you listening to country music before you moved to Nashville?

Believe it or not, I have always loved country music. I mean, when everybody wanted to play rock 'n' roll, I always loved country music. I don't know what it was. I got involved in it because my parents listened to it a lot. I was aware of it. I was one of those guys who would do whatever it took to make some money and become a better drummer. So I played polkas, country gigs, anything. It was all about learning to be a better drummer, and making money to pay the bills. It never bothered me to play a brush/stick shuffle and see how good I could make it feel. I loved the challenge of trying to sound like Buddy Harman playing with Ray Price. "Can I do this? What can I do to please the people that I'm working for? Because I really want to work." It was always about trying to please the musicians and bandleaders so I could work steady. That was my ultimate goal.

I never wanted to work real steady for a month and then be laid off. I had an attitude of wanting to stay with a band as long as I could. I didn't want to jump to another band to earn fifteen dollars more a night or whatever. I always wanted to stay until it didn't work to stay long and not burn any bridges. Improving as a drummer was always important.

Country music, yes . . . I've never been asked that before. I've just always liked three-quarter time. I didn't have any problem wanting to do that. I never came here thinking I was going to be the next big session player. I didn't know how good I was, but I knew that I was good enough as a solid person, staying punctual, and able to play well. I knew that I could certainly get a job. The thing that really got me was sessions. The very first session I did in Nashville (jumping ahead a little bit to show you where I'm coming from), I got through my wife, who was signed to a record deal. Her name is Marlys Roe. She was in a really big R&B band in South Dakota and had a regional hit up there that was produced in California. Glen D. Hardin played on it, and Sonny Curtis produced it. When she came to Nashville, she got a record deal.

I got to play on the session. Well, let me tell ya somethin', whew! It was Bob Moore on acoustic bass, Pig Robbins on piano. I believe it was Grady Martin on electric guitar, Pete Drake on steel guitar. . . . All these great "A" players. It was just a waltz. I'd played it a hundred times, but on the rundown it sounded like a record! I was wondering what I should play, and they were popping out parts so fast! At that moment I had two things going through my mind: One, "Wow! What am I doing here?" And two, "What can I do to stay here?" It was just a simple waltz with a dotted rhythm. I teach my granddaughter to play that, but the pressure of being in there with those guys that can do it perfectly just like having a conversation without having to work it out . . . My emotions were mixed. I knew that I had to do something to do that all the time.

I got through the session okay. I got better after that. I had recorded before, but it was typical band stuff. It was good, but, my God, you get in there with guys and two to three hours later you're still going over the same song. It's just a nightmare. These guys [the "A Team"] come and introduce themselves—it's like, "Hi, how are ya?" The pianist quickly says he's going to play something [for a part], everybody's running with ideas, and I'm thinking, "Excuse me? Where should I play my bass drum?" [laughs].

They didn't really talk too much. I'm sure that they were wondering where Buddy Harman was. I was there because Neil Wilburn was producing and he believed in me. He wouldn't have put me in there if he didn't think that I could do it. At the same time, I wasn't and never will be Buddy Harman. He [Harman] was a hero of mine as a person and player. So they gave me the cold shoulder a little.

It worked out great, though. I remember walking by Grady Martin. He was very famous but could really put a chink in your armor if he wanted to. I was afraid of him. I was still wondering how I did and had to walk past him tuning up. I can't remember exactly what he said, but I was scared of getting hammered by him, but he said, "Hey kid. Don't let them give you any crap. You play good." Wow! Oh, man! I couldn't believe he said that. That was a huge boost for me. It was such a confidence builder. I didn't think I was Buddy Rich after that, but it was great to know that an unbelievable musician thinks that I've got what it takes.

I had moments like that over the course of my life—confidence builders. Myron [Lee] gave me my first opportunity with a seasoned band. Although their big touring years were over, I learned a lot about the music business from him—how to make the right moves, money things, and other things that really helped me. My father told me that he believed I had what it took to be a professional musician. All those things meant a lot to me.

To rewind a little bit , you got married and told her that you were going to move to Nashville. What did day one in town and the next little bit look like?

Well, like I said, I had been here briefly in 1969 and it was a disaster because the connections I made didn't pan out. It happens that people tell you to call them when you get into town, and when you do, they either don't have any idea who you are or they don't have anything to offer. When you're young, it's easy to get enamored with the idea of being in Nashville.

So I told my wife that we needed to move, and she agreed. We put our house up for sale, put the dog in the car, and loaded the U-Haul trailer. There was quite a bit of apprehension there. We were leaving our family, the band had found another club gig, and, really, leaving a normal life behind. We played six nights a week. In the summer, we had a softball team. We had a basketball team, played golf, and rode dirt bikes together. It was the perfect family.

We were nervous seeing Sioux City in the rearview mirror. It wasn't far down the road when we knew we were making the right decision. I don't want to be corny, but it was almost like God planned it for us. We weren't very spiritual at the time, but as I look back, God had this planned for me because the worst day of my life turned out to be the best—when the band got fired in Sioux City. If we had stayed there any longer and had children, we wouldn't have left. When you get locked into that security, you don't push yourself.

Even though I had been here before, I didn't have any connections. The first day in town, we went to a motel on Murfreesboro Road called the Alamo. My wife went out looking for apartments and found one about a week later on Edmonson Pike. We moved in on December 14. Every Monday, I went downtown at nine o'clock as if I had a gig. I visited places like Demon's Den on lower Broadway, where a lot of the touring musicians hung out, and sat in. They had a house band. It was a funky little dive. We call it a "skull orchard" because it isn't there anymore.

I went there and didn't speak to anybody the first week. I got a Coke—I don't drink [alcohol]—and just watched. I didn't introduce myself or try to get a gig. The next week, one of the guys approached me, asked if I was a musician, and invited me to sit in. I said I would if I knew the song. I started sitting in pretty often. After about two weeks, a guy from Nat Stuckey's band said he [Stuckey] was looking for a drummer and asked if I wanted the gig. I said, "Sure." That was in February.

Typically, as it used to be, a lot of the *Grand Ole Opry* stars didn't work in the winter. They just did the Opry and stayed at home. Nat happened to work thirteen days that month and quite a few more dates through April. It was only fifty dollars a night, but thirteen gigs was good. Our apartment rent wasn't much, and we had a bit of a nest egg, so we were quickly making ends meet. It was great. That's how I got going.

How long did that gig last?
I was probably with him for two or three months. I got asked to play in Printer's Alley with Jim Vest and the Nashville Cats through another connection. That was a *big* deal. It was six nights a week and paid $125 a week. The gig was from nine p.m. to two a.m. I got to back up a lot of country artists that came in there. I really learned to hone my country skills to play really traditional and solid. I got a lot of custom sessions from that. It helped a lot.

Were you still using the Rogers kit?

Yes. I need to tell you something first: When I moved into the Edmonson Pike apartment, the very first day that I paid the rent, she said, "Oh, we have another drummer that lives here. His name is Larrie Londin." I didn't know Larrie, but she said that we should get together. She gave me his apartment number. A little time went by, and Larrie and I became really good friends.

I would go over to his house, have sandwiches, and hang out. In fact, Larrie did a lot of great things for all of us [drummers]. Two things that stand out the most is his lending me his car and snare drum to go play my first session. I only had one car, and I got called out of the blue to do a two o'clock session at Hilltop Studios. I wasn't expecting the call, and my wife had the car.

I got on my first number one hit record because of him. He was recording Mel Tillis's record with Jimmy Bowen producing. Larrie was doing something else when he got called for the session and recommended me. Jimmy didn't want to use me, but Larrie assured him that I could handle it. The record was "I Believe in You" (1978). Jim Horn and Joe Osborn played on it, plus a bunch of other great players.

So, back to Printer's Alley, that was a tremendous gig for a couple of years. Larrie was playing at the Carousel Club two doors down. We had breakfast every night. He would tell me what was going on, what I needed to do, and the next thing I know he recommended me for Ray Stevens's job. I auditioned for Ray, got the gig, and I was with him from 1974 through July 1979. In the meantime, I started doing a lot more sessions.

I quit Printer's Alley because I couldn't do a six p.m. session and make the gig because it started at nine p.m. I gave up working steady at Printer's Alley to work with Ray, who worked a couple times a week. The money was just a little bit better, but it wasn't as steady. We might work but then be off for a while. That first year was a little bit scary. I started working more demos and then a few more master recordings. The big decision came in July 1979.

I was starting to get more calls for sessions. Stevens wasn't working that much, but we would occasionally do a week in Las Vegas or something. I remember one time we went on the road, and I called home to ask my wife if anybody called. She said that Billy Sherrill had called asking if I was available for George Jones, Tammy Wynette, and some other big sessions. I hated to miss those. It was one thing to miss a demo, but these were big records. I told her that I had to make a decision to pursue sessions full-time, otherwise they weren't going to call me. Back then, you really couldn't go on the road without it hurting your session career. They didn't think you were taking it seriously. She said it was okay if I did.

I turned in my notice and became dependent on the telephone. Oh, boy, that was scary. All of a sudden, there was no money from Ray [Stevens] and everything that came in to pay the bills was a telephone call. At first, it was very tense. By the second year, I had gained back the money I had lost from touring. After that, within a couple of years, it turned into the best decision I made. I loved working for Ray. He is a wonderful person and talent. I just wanted to play on sessions ever since that wonderful experience I talked about earlier. Also, all of the demos and custom records I had done since that point confirmed my love for recording.

I love the creative process of recording. It is so neat to sit around the studio and look around to see all the talent sitting around. I remember all the gospel and country records we did here [the Ruckus Room] and all the fun we had in this room. The process is so uplifting and exciting, even if it's a simple beat.

Here's the deal, country music now allows for the drummer to play a lot. You can almost play whatever you want. It's like seventies rock 'n' roll—no offense [laughs]. When I started, you were really limited to brush and stick. Then Larrie Londin came along and started the half-time thing and slamming on the drums a little more. Then we got to start to bring our own drums to the studio instead of using a house kit. It allowed for more individual personality. The guys playing today get to have a lot of fun.

When I was playing, it was literally about not playing too much. Larrie was such a wonderful person. If there was a song where they didn't want you to play the snare drum until the second chorus, he would explain to me how to get that done. I'd complain that I didn't know what to do. He'd talk me through a bunch of ideas using the hi-hat or cross stick and paint this picture of how to make music without really playing. He had this way with *space*. I will always love him for the way he mentored me and many other drummers.

I've always liked all phases of Nashville and the music. Today you have all these wonderful players. The sounds are great, and everything is very good musically. I like the music that's going on. I can see why people are coming to town to play country music. It wasn't like that back then with the drummer up front. I'm sure you've seen how things have changed from brushes to brushes and stick, to half-time, to rockabilly, to rock 'n' roll now. It's an exciting time.

What were some of the studios you were working in at the time?

Once I got busy doing a lot of sessions—and I'm talking about days with sessions at ten, two, six, and ten, as often as I could physically and emotionally handle it—you just play all over. I worked most places that were on Music Row—Columbia, RCA, and all those other places. There were a lot of studios in Franklin and Hendersonville and Bradley's Barn. Quadraphonic is great.

Franklin really got a lot of studios later in the 1980s. The Bennett house was down there. David Briggs had a studio. Monument studio was great. Wherever there was work, if you were one of the guys, you worked there.

Which rooms were your favorites?

I don't know if I had a favorite room, because I have such an appreciation for the guys turning the knobs. Ron "Snake" Reynolds was one of the best engineers that I've ever worked with. We did all of the Earl Thomas Conley stuff, we recorded Billy Joe Royal's (who wrote "Down in the Boondocks") comeback, and a bunch of other stuff. He was one of the best.

What did Reynolds bring to the table?

I'll tell you exactly what he brought to the table: the playback sounded like the radio. It was hyped up with volume. It was a combination of power and quality. That's what he brought. The headphone mix made you want to play. The playback mix made you want to play even more. Believe it or not, I'm probably not qualified to talk a lot about this because I don't know the technology. All I know is that Snake, and several others certainly, made you really want to play up to the sound you were hearing.

We would do a project like Earl Thomas Conley's, who may have been the first artist to have four number one records off the same album, and we couldn't wait to get to the session early and hear his rough mix of what we did the previous day. It was exciting. You *wanted* to play. In my opinion, it's easier to get a good sound now than it was back in the old days. I don't think the gear was as sophisticated. From what I understand with all the ProTools technology, I have been in people's houses that are not great studios and got an incredible sound because of the gear and plug-ins.

I love to be in a room full of warm bodies and be creative. That's why I don't have a home studio with people sending me stuff. I'm not smart enough for that [laughs], and I have the luxury of saying what I will and won't do. If that's what it will take for me to work, I won't do it. I want the experience of being behind drums, seeing a band, and looking at the artist.

There were a lot of studios where I really had to work hard to get a good sound. There was a boxy sound because of the single-headed toms and carpeted walls. There were some guys like Snake that could really get a good sound regardless of, or in spite of, the room.

Who else falls into that category of engineer?

Brent King! In fact, I just worked with him about four or five months ago on a contemporary Christian project at Ronnie Milsap's old studio. I hadn't seen him in a long time. Wow! It was like I'd forgotten how good he is. I always get myself in trouble in these interviews. I want to be honest but I don't want to offend anybody. There appears to be a lot of people that come out of recording schools that can just fly on a computer. They can cut and paste and whatever, but they just don't seem to have the ears when it comes to recording a whole band together. Every now and then, you'll run into somebody that gets all the modern stuff but has the ears of an older guy that doesn't go by the book.

Some of the young engineers—and I say this with all due respect because I don't want to sound like the old, bitter guy because I've been blessed—don't really bring things to life like Snake, Brent, and the other guys. Billy Sherrill, not the producer, is another engineer that just makes things sound incredible.

A lot of guys don't seem to have that. I don't know what it is because I'm not qualified to say. It's just, as a player, you know when it's right when you put the headphones on and can hear everything without having to overplay. Then you hear the playback and you can hear every subtle thing that you did. It makes you want to do cool things because you know it isn't going to get lost.

There was a time in our lives when we were playing big John Guerin–type kits. Of course, engineers didn't know how to handle them. I learned big Elton John–type fills from Larrie Londin. If the engineer wasn't very sharp, you'd only hear the accents, and it sounded strange. So you'd have to change how you'd play because you know subtle things wouldn't get heard, which meant playing really hard, sparse, and open. If I didn't compensate, it would sound stupid.

That sounds like it would require a strong retention and adaptability.

Yes! And the great players have that. If you're at a particular studio like this one, it's amazing how good things can sound with the gear that they have. Players probably don't have to compensate so much anymore because of the sophistication of the gear. Back then, we'd learn from the headphones or playback that we'd have to hit the snare drum harder, forget about playing a certain tom because it wasn't coming through, avoid any busy tom fills, or whatever. You always had to think about what was and wasn't going to make the record.

Talking about recording studios, though, the Berry Hill area was—well, still is—another place that has been around for quite a while. I worked a lot out here. The studio that I worked at a lot is right down around the corner. It was Randy Scruggs's place. I worked a lot for a producer named Nelson Larkin who did the Billy Joe Royal and Earl Thomas Conley stuff. I used to work at Buzz Cason's studio, which is also right around the corner. Buzz's second studio is now called Blackbird, which is owned by Martina McBride and her husband. Of course, that's where Eddie Bayers did all of the Judds' stuff. Treasure Isle is a couple blocks down. I did a lot of gospel work there. There is a lot of work in Berry Hill. It was well established when I came to town, but a lot more of the studios came in the 1980s when they bought all of the houses.

There was a very popular studio called Reflections. It was a really good place to play, and I'm sure it still is. I don't know the history, but I heard about it being bought and doing a lot of in-house work.

Did you see a lot of the same players on sessions?

Well, I have to back up a second. When you first start, you're the new kid on the block and all you are trying to do is work. That's another thing that I learned. I don't know how I knew this, or why I felt this, but it really helped me.

When I moved to town, I didn't show up like a roaring wind saying, "Look who's here." I stayed quiet. I was scared a little bit. I was overwhelmed a little bit, but I still had a desire to succeed no matter what. When I would meet people, I would never push myself or, I guess the word is network. I'd never say, "Hey Tony, I'm Jerry Kroon. Man, if you've got some work . . ." and wear you out.

I learned a lot by watching people and listening to what made people angry. People that came on too strong would turn people off. When I would meet people, I would tell them that I was new to town and was looking for work if they asked me. I never said that I was in town to be the next Buddy Harman, Jerry Carrigan, or Larrie Londin. The cool thing, however it got started, once I had done a few sessions, I would get calls to sub for Jerry Carrigan. He's an unbelievable session drummer.

When he would call me to sub for him, I would play his drums. I mean, he once called me for a "Me and My RC" commercial that paid me residuals for almost a year. If he was sick or whatever, I would let him know that I really appreciated him and let him know that I was going to keep the seat warm for him until he got back. It was important to me that he knew that I wasn't trying to steal his gig. Also, in those situations, I did my best to sound as close to his style as possible and play in a manner that made it sound like he was there.

Tommy Wells would call me to sub for him if he was busy. All I wanted to do was do a good job and keep the seat warm until he got back. I never wanted to steal their gigs. I didn't want a gig unless I either earned it or it was the right way to get it. I didn't want to BS my way into saying things like, "You need to call me because somebody's sick all the time." My attitude was to consider how to please the person I'm working for and let Jerry know that everything went well. That really helped me a lot. I pushed myself, but I tried not to go overboard and be overbearing with it. I'm sure some people would disagree, but that happens.

I know at times I believed my own P.R., and somebody knocked me down a peg or two. At those times, I apologized and moved on. Initially,

I knew what people were thinking because I had gotten that cold shoulder from the "A Team" when I did my wife's session. I just worked my way up, biding my time, and it was great. I had a wonderful run. I can't believe it.

My goal was this: I was hoping to make a living playing drums. Once I started playing sessions, that's all I wanted to do. It's still my favorite thing. I'd rather do that than play live. Maybe growing up and playing in clubs soured me to it. I'm not knocking anybody that likes that, but it just isn't for me anymore. I was hoping that by the time that it all came to an end, I was ready to be done without regrets. I have some minor regrets—it's impossible not to—but I had a great time.

In 2003, I had a terrible thing happen. I lost my fine motor skills in my right hand due to focal dystonia. It happens to about 1 percent of musicians. I knew something was wrong when I was practicing. I used to practice all the time. Monday through Friday was all about music to me. I didn't mow the lawn or wash the car. On the weekend, it was family time. I guarantee you, though, that if I didn't have a session on a weekday, I spent two to three hours practicing.

Anyway, I was practicing one day. I was doing some linear things, and my hand was slow. I couldn't figure out what was going on. To make a long story short, I realized I had some sort of problem. I had a neurologist check it out, and she discovered that I had this condition. She said that it wasn't too bad, but it will continue to get worse. I took my pension in 2003, but the union allows me to play a certain dollar amount worth of sessions before I have to stop. So I continue to do as much as I can without affecting my pension.

When I hit the first lick, my hand wants to release the stick. I can't play the Purdie or Porcaro sixteenth notes anymore. I'll be sixty-five years old in October [2011], and I notice that it gets a little worse each year. I practice to work around my condition, and sometimes play a traditional grip in my right hand. I can play fills that way. If it's a loud rock 'n' roll sound, I can play with matched grip because that's just quarter notes.

It's become quite a mental process of dealing with it. I looked back on the years that I had. I realized that I couldn't go as hard as I used to, so I had to start phasing out some work to keep from being in a position where I wasn't able to give the client and fellow musicians the right feel. I didn't want to be in a position where I was making excuses for my playing.

I still play with Don McLean and am able to do that. In fact, I turned down some pretty good sessions this year because I knew in my heart that I would really have to think about my limitations. That isn't any fun, so I just tell them, "No, thank you." That's where I'm at these days.

So with all that being said [laughs], I didn't answer your question about the other players. Basically, when you first start working, you work for anybody. Then, somewhere along the line, you develop a group of guys that branch out from doing custom sessions or whatever. You get producers that like certain players, and you start seeing them two to three times a week. Maybe one of them plays on a record and recommends you for a date. There was a group of people that I probably played with more than any others. At one time or another, I probably worked with everybody.

My group worked together quite a bit. It isn't really a clique, but there's a chemistry there. Before Eddie Bayers Jr. started doing bigger records, he was working at Audio Media Studios with Paul Worley (guitar) and Dennis Burnside (piano). That little section was great. If memory serves me right, I think Jim Ed Norman heard them working as a group and wanted them on an Anne Murray record. I think of the Muscle Shoals rhythm section or the Wrecking Crew as examples of the way players gravitate toward each other.

When I played on hit records, I'd see one or two of my crew. We didn't record a lot of big records together, but we did a lot of work. I usually saw Gary Prim on piano, Sonny Garrish on steel guitar, and David Smith or Larry Paxton on bass. If you had several "blue chip" accounts, you'd see the same guys on those. Paxton, Garrish, and a piano player that is now deceased named Mitch Humphries. We did the Vern Gosdin records. We did many records at RCA with that crew.

Yeah, there's a core group, but there are a lot of circles. You get called for a lot of record dates, maybe some custom accounts (people that aren't signed to a major label that want to make a record), and some gospel accounts. I did a lot of work with [producer] Kevin McManus, and my core group was there. I know that at our busiest, we'd see each other two or three times a week.

There were times when you wouldn't see any of them. On that session that I mentioned with Brent King earlier, I saw four people that I see consistently. However, there were three others that I almost never see.

Do you feel like there was a special chemistry with that core group?

When you're good, you're good. It's like this: let's say it's Monday morning and I've got a ten o'clock session. The drums show up early, and I've got my sounds by 9:30 a.m. Then the room fills up with players. I might be working with a guitar player or bass player that I haven't seen in a while, but by the time we play the first song, I know him. I might not know his kids, or the food he likes, but the music thread is there. You don't really need to *know* the guy personally. You just need to know how it sounds in the control room, that it's comfortable, and that he isn't difficult to be around.

Let's say you get into a session that requires some heavy lifting, that has a player or leader that dictates everything. That isn't any fun. I think you could take complete strangers that have never played together, but are great musicians, and have a good session. I think the difference with working with a core group of guys is that you tend to know them so well that you aren't thinking at all about what the other player is going to do. You know it's going to be right. You don't have to talk.

If you work with somebody that you don't know, you may realize that what you normally do musically isn't working. It probably isn't the new player's fault, but the communication isn't as strong. The difference between a strong core of players and strangers is you know where everybody is going even though you haven't heard the song yet.

I know during a ritard, for example, that Gary Prim slows down a certain way. I know what I can do to subdivide in between his notes and how he is going to feel it. We don't need to rehearse it. At the same time, I have worked with new people and somehow, in a heartbeat, we understand each other. It might be a mutual respect for talent where you yield to their thing.

Larry Paxton is a great bass player. We never had to talk. If you were interviewing Larry, he'd say that he isn't concerned about talking things out. He just wants to play, and he's right. I don't have to talk to him about my bass drum pattern for part of a song. He just figures it out when we get there [laughs].

I'm not sure I answered your question or not, but I do think there is an advantage to working with guys all the time, especially if you're under a time crunch. There are some sessions that one song might get done in three hours. Other sessions, like a custom session, have a budget that requires four songs in three hours, and they need to sound like you only did one. They need quality and quantity. Those sessions need people that can take direction, assume responsibilities, and come up with ideas very quickly without depending on somebody to say what to play.

Gary Prim is a great session leader, and Sonny Garrish is the same way. If Gary is the leader on a session, he'll just look at Sonny and say, "How about you play an intro here?" and, boom, that's done. There might be a few more suggestions, we'll run it down, and then play the song. That's it. Gary is the kind of leader that you can suggest things to him too. He isn't on an ego trip.

You get the heavy lifting when somebody comes in and tells you every note to play. I always felt like telling a guy like that to take the drum sticks and play it himself. You know, "I've got to go home and floss the dog's teeth."

Yeah, it turns into a situation where you've been working for three hours, you look at your watch, and you've only been there five minutes.

Exactly [laughs]! Yeah, I had dark hair when the session started [laughs].

Thank God that I didn't have a lot of those. That's a side of the session business that people don't like to talk about, but it exists.

The bottom line, to answer your question, is that there is an advantage to knowing the people you're working with. It helps to get the groove going, you know what they're going to do, but, oddly enough, it's never boring! You know, there is a formula to music. If you say to me that we've got ten songs to do, and I've got nine hours, or even six hours, to get them done . . . Some people have small budgets, but they want the same quality as a Michael W. Smith record that may have spent three hours on a song. There are a lot of records out there that are recorded in six hours. In those situations, it helps to have a group of guys that you know. On the other hand, if a player is in the Nashville mode, the session should go well.

If you've got a good song, a good singer, the studio sounds great, and everybody can play, it won't take long to get a great product.

Do you have any favorite sessions or records?

That's a really difficult question. I think the ones that stand out for me are the ones that had an experienced artist. For example, Earl Thomas Conley started out as ETC Band. We cut his record as an independent record at Quad Studios. He got picked up by RCA and went from being ETC Band to Earl Thomas Conley the superstar.

The first George Strait sessions that I did were great. He was a new artist that never had a hit record. I don't want to sound egotistical, but it was really great to be playing on the record of an unknown one day and all of a sudden see him on billboards. There is no feeling like working with an artist, hearing him on the radio, and knowing that you had a small part in it. It's really satisfying to watch a song climb the charts, maybe go to number one, and then turning into either a gold or platinum album. It isn't like you're Buddy Rich, or anybody like that, but it's great to be a part of the process. In my career, I hoped to be involved in things like that.

Another great record was Terri Gibbs's "Somebody's Knockin'." Terri Gibbs was a blind piano player that was working in a piano bar in Augusta, Georgia. I don't know how she got signed to a record deal up here. She came in. It was her first time in a studio. "Somebody's Knockin'" was a huge hit for her. She went from playing a piano bar to selling eight hundred thousand or a million records.

Sammy Kershaw had a song called "Cadillac Style." We were at Harold's Shed Studio on a Monday morning, at least I think it was, at ten o'clock. We were all set up and this new guy is coming in. Harold is producing. Of course, he had produced Alabama and others. At this point in our careers, we were a little bit jaded. We were out drinking coffee and it got to be around eleven o'clock. We got to wondering what was going on, wanting to get on with the session. Sammy still hadn't shown up. So we started getting impatient asking where he was. We heard that he was a good singer, and it was a Master session, so we wanted to get on with it.

Another hour or so later, a brand new pickup pulls in with the side all banged up. It was Sammy. He had driven all night long from Louisiana. He fell asleep on a bridge, scraped up the side of his truck, and that's why he was late. He came in, opened his mouth, and started singing. We were like, "Wow!" The next thing you know, "Cadillac Style" goes number one. Then he had a gold record and album.

Being a session player, it's one thing to work a lot and it's another thing to play on great songs. It was great to provide for my family and work, but I was happy to play on hit records. I can remember saying, "Man, I'm working in Printer's Alley. If I could just do one demo a week, that would be great." That turned into wanting to do two or three demos and a gig. Of course, that turns into wanting to just do one master recording. It just keeps building. You know, "If I could just do three master's a week . . ." And on and on.

I can't tell you anything that I've done musically that I'm proud of that is outstanding like Gadd playing "50 Ways to Leave Your Lover." I've never been able to do that, nor have I been put in that kind of situation. I did get to provide some nice grooves, tasty licks, and be solid enough to play on some records. I was happy with that. I'm not a drummer's drummer.

If I went over and played that drum set over there by myself, you'd be bored in five minutes. I do think I had an ability to play a song and pick out tasty places to play, drive it hard when it was necessary, and am a very good ballad player. I always enjoyed playing ballads. I had great ideas for fills that were musical, I thought. I can base that on the fact that people kept calling. I enjoyed the creative process of making records, whether that was making "boom, chick" as great as it could be or whatever.

Do you have a favorite ballad that you recorded?

I can't think of any right now. I always like the kinds of ballads that had real open fills with flams on multiple toms. This is going to sound really strange to you, but my joy and happiness in the studio came from creating a part of anything that had a good feel, good fills, and was played well. If the singer, producer, and players were happy, and if I didn't rush, drag, or do something stupid, I was happy.

Your discography has a Ray Charles record on it. How did that come about?

That was an album where Ray Charles wanted to do some things in Nashville. He used some different singers. I think the song I played on was a duet with Janie Fricke. Unfortunately, he was not at the session. I remember that we cut the song, and he was going to fly in and do the vocals. That's the way that whole album went. It was a compilation thing.

Janie Fricke was a great singer. I have a funny story about her from one of my earlier sessions. She is a terrific singer, but she was a famous background and jingle singer before she was famous. She was all over television and radio singing on jingles and hits singing background. She got a deal as an artist. I got called for her first album, before she really had a strong direction. I think a lot of her success can be attributed to Bob Montgomery's production when the hits started happening.

Anyway, this is not her first time in the studio, obviously. Everything she sang was great. We were at Columbia Room B. We had a room full of great players like Pig Robbins, Bob Moore, Pete Drake, and all those guys, plus some string players and background singers. The string arranger was Bill Justis.

I was feeling pretty good. I was past the early session jitters. I had some credibility as a player at that point. I had the attitude that I could play "on the edge" a little bit. I think I had eight-inch, ten-inch, twelve-inch, and fourteen-inch toms on my drum set. So, like I said, she didn't really have a direction, so we were experimenting. One side of the album was kind of country, and the other side was kind of like Barbara Streisand with some big ballads and cool stuff.

Like I said, I was feeling good that day [laughs], so I played this fill that I just nailed! I just ripped it out! We got done, and I was proud of myself. I was trying to be more aggressive. A quiet came over the session. I hear the playback over these big speakers, and the producer said, "Geez! Who's the hippie drummer that thinks he's playing with Blood, Sweat, and Tears?" I just put my head in my hands. Then I hear, "Awww, just kidding ya! That sounded great!" Everybody was laughing. I got hung out to dry. I folded up like a cheap tent because my confidence was shot.

You did a lot of work with Willie Nelson.

Willie is an interesting guy. Do you know what I found out in my career? The bigger the star, the nicer they are. There are exceptions to the rule, but it's mostly true. I worked on an album with Dolly Parton years ago. She was the nicest person. Willie was the same way. He was great. There was never a problem with Willie.

We went to Austin, Texas, to record a duet with Willie Nelson and Faron Young. They are old friends. They go back years. A bunch of us went to Willie's studio. Fred Foster was producing it. It was me, Steve Gibson, and Mike Leech. We were there about a week.

We worked at the studio from about five p.m., every day, for three or four hours, and then went out to eat. The next day we'd go play some golf on Willie's course. Back at the studio, Willie would just kind of saunter in with a bottle of tequila with the worm in it. He and Faron would get at each other like an old married couple. It was just a great time. There was never any ego or anything. We just played and it was great!

Most of the big stars that I worked with were just the nicest people. You can't find a nicer guy than George Strait. The posers, the up-and-comers that believe their P.R., are the ones that would usually give you a lot of problems.

Without naming names, what would a problem on a session look like?

Funny thing, I had a situation in this studio one time. We were cutting—I have to be careful here—an album. The artist was an established country star that had a few hits. We worked all day, and everything was going fine until the last song. We cut the last song, we go to listen to the playback, and there's unhappiness written all over the man's face.

So obviously we were there to please and want to try to make the artist happy. We come back out, record the song again, and we get, "You guys just aren't getting it. I don't know what's wrong? Drummer! What are you playing?" I had been here nine hours, and he's calling me "Drummer"? So I explain, and he's still unhappy.

We played it again, go to the control room for the playback, and he's still complaining! I finally had enough and said, "Buddy, this isn't exactly top shelf material we're cutting here!" And it wasn't because the other eight songs or whatever were just as smooth as silk. He was telling us that we were awesome all day long. How do you go from, "Man, you guys are incredible! It sounds great! You are making me so happy! Thank you for being on my record!" to treating us like we can't play? He wasn't even calling us by our names anymore and was treating us like we were nothing. Well, it turns out that he had written the song and it was terrible [all of the other songs were written by other songwriters]. That's why it wasn't feeling good. There was nothing to it, and I had had enough.

So the song was finished at that point?

[laughs] Boy, I guess so! Yeah. Well, I got fired from the session. It was going on one a.m., and all of a sudden he started to jerk our chain. It would have been one thing if he had been like that all day, but how do you do that? It would be like if I turned on you right now. You'd wonder where that came from.

I'll tell you something else, and this is going to be out of context, but to go back to the nice people in the session world. Do you remember the writing team of Burt Bacharach and Hal David?

Yes.

Cool. Hal David came to Nashville years ago to produce an artist. I got called to do the session, and I was blown away by the opportunity. He's such a fantastic writer. I wasn't sure I could pull it off, but I had to!

We were at a studio that was near Quadraphonic. I mean, this is *the* Hal David. We were cutting the record, and he said the coolest thing. You know, when we finish a take, we go in to listen back. We're side-men, but we're also producers. We don't take credit for it, but we like to make sure our part is gelling and make sure that everybody is happy. You know how it is. You aren't brown nosing; you're just checking your part because if the record doesn't sell you don't want it to be about you. It's quality control, and 99 percent of the players are that way. We don't go sit down and say, "If you find something wrong, call me."

So Hal said to us after a couple of sessions, "You guys are amazing! You guys listen to the song after each take all the way through. I'm not used to that." He wasn't putting down New York players by any means, but the general idea we got from him was that they would read the chart, do a few takes, and allow the producer to piece together the song from what they had. They play what's written, and they're great at it. We were much more vocal about our ideas, like suggesting a half-time feel or chord change. He was blown away by that. It was really neat. The point I'm making is that a man of his stature, that has worked with the caliber of players that he has, came to town and appreciated what we did as Nashville musicians. It was very neat to me. He was a wonderful guy. There was no ego, and he wasn't hard-nosed at all.

As session musicians in this town, we understand that sometimes the guy writing the chart doesn't always understand what's going to work on a country song. Just because a writer loves the music doesn't mean he can write every note, so we're happy to give our input. I'm a good R&B, rock, and country player, but I can't play jazz like it should be, although I love it. Hal was just wonderful about taking suggestions. So I've found that the biggest stars I've worked with are confident, trust the players, and make you feel good.

You played on a lot of Gospel records and did a lot with Bill Gaither.

Bill Gaither was a wonderful guy to work for. Gosh, I had five to seven years of work with Bill. I played on some of his stuff and a lot of the Homecoming things. I don't know if you know what those are. He has this deal where he'll go and put on a concert with the Gaither Vocal Band and several gospel artists that will do one or two songs. It's an amazing thing. I went to one of the shows when they were here and didn't know what to expect, and it was great. People really get their money's worth with all of the people there singing.

Bill really loves southern gospel music and can go way back. He can tell you who sang on a song from the 1940s. He was a student of it. He was a wonderful guy to work for. He treated everybody with respect. He spent a lot of time in the studio. It isn't because he's so technically musical. It's just that he would communicate with his hands and get his point across. I loved the man and was eager to give him anything he needed. He has been wonderful for that genre of music. I would like to say that Bill Gaither is responsible for keeping southern gospel alive and in the forefront because of the shows that he's done and the Homecoming events that showcased so many artists. He's a wonderful guy.

We should also talk about your relationship with Ricky Skaggs.

Oh, yeah! Boy, that was great. Ricky Skaggs's *Waiting for the Sun to Shine*. I did not play on "Highway 40 Blues," which was the hit, but I did do about half of the album. For some reason, Ricky wanted to use me. It was me and Joe Osborn and, I think, Lloyd Green. We did a lot of traditional country things, and it was a wonderful album to play on. I think I got a gold or platinum [record] out of it.

Ricky is a tremendous musician. He's very particular about what he wants—especially concerning tempo. I really enjoyed working with him. It was a wonderful project. I think at that time, if I'm not mistaken, he was into bluegrass and was moving into country music. After that, he went on to have several more great country hits. I didn't play on them, but it was a real joy to work with him.

I'm sixty-five years old, I have a bad arm, and my goal is still to grow up and be a drummer. I came from a small farm town in South Dakota with no formal training. I love music, and I got into music knowing that I wanted to do it for a living. I want to give God credit for the career that I had. I look back and analyze how I got to where I did, and I really think I was meant to be where I was. I came to Nashville. I was good but not the best. I raised my family, and I was blessed to play on a lot of records. I played the cards that were dealt to me, and I never stopped working on my playing.

I was never totally happy with the way I played. I'm critical to a fault in regards to my playing. I had the confidence to do certain things and push the boundaries to make myself a better player. I believe that God gives a person an amount of talent, and this is what was doled out to me.

When I say that I wasn't that great of a player, I mean that I can't do the things my heroes did. I wanted to be a player so bad that I kept working at it. At the end of the day, I took somebody (me) from a small town and played with some of the best in the world. I got a lot of respect from the musicians and raised my family. I can't ask for any more than that.

We talked about Larrie Londin, Steve Gadd, and Jeff Porcaro briefly. Who were some of the drummers that you were listening to for inspiration?

This is going to sound weird, but just about everybody that played the instrument. If you asked me right now who I would be if I could be any drummer, I would be happy to be Steve Gadd or Jeff Porcaro. Those are my two favorite players because they were the ultimate studio players who could play anything.

Another guy that I really like because he could do any music style is Carlos Vega. You know he used to come to Nashville to do sessions. He had such a light, easy touch, and you could hear him on a jazz thing or whatever.

I was never a jazz or fusion-type player. I never had experience with that. I love jazz. In fact, Bob Mater is one of my favorite jazz players. I've always loved his playing. He is so right on with it. He *knows* what to do. It's just second nature to him. He's a friend of mine that has always been supportive of me and my playing. I did a few swing albums with a steel player. I've always wanted to do that really well but never had enough experience with it. I didn't grow up playing in that style.

When I was growing up, I tried to learn the parts so I could be in a band. If that meant I was playing like Ringo Starr, so be it. At that point, I didn't really idolize anybody. I was just trying to survive. I knew early on that I wasn't the most gifted. I really had to work at it. I'm not saying that other people don't work hard, but I think I had to break it down a lot more than my friends who played drums.

The key for me was playing with those bands in South Dakota. Those guys had worked with better players than me, and they were always pushing me. They told me that I sounded like I was building a house behind the drum set. They called me a "fair weather player" because I only played well a few times a year. Seriously, I had no confidence, but I really found myself when I started recording. That's when I learned that I could play and sound good. I didn't have to play a thirty-second note roll, but I could make a backbeat in a ballad sound great.

So I found myself. In the meantime, I never stopped trying to listen to everybody. I did gravitate toward Gadd for his swampy R&B thing. I loved Jeff [Porcaro] for his precise fills, groove, and those ultimate Bernard Purdie parts, and the feel! There are so many people that you can listen to that I just had to hone it down to one or two guys that really capture what it means to be a great drummer. It seems like when I listen to Porcaro, Gadd, and Carlos [Vega] that their styles just fit into everything that they did. They were so awesome.

I figured that if I listened to them and could get an idea of what they were thinking, maybe I could transfer it into some country thing I was doing. You and I were talking about fills—I love that Nigel Olsson/Elton John–type drumming with those open, spacy fills. Larrie Londin played those kinds of fills early in his career. I grooved on that kind of stuff.

I can't even go to the NAMM Show anymore because those guys play more sitting down in five minutes than I did in a year. It's overwhelming. I got to a mind-set that I stopped trying to be the guys that were hot and asked the Lord to let me be me.

Somebody told me some good advice one time. He said, "At some point, you just need to start playing like you and trust that." There's already a Steve Gadd or Vinnie Colaiuta. They are wonderful, but hearing that advice really helped me. Prior to that advice, I was bouncing around all the time. For me, that can be detrimental because I didn't know who I was.

Once I got better in the studio, I played like me. Yes, you hired me and I'm going to do everything I can to give you what you want as a producer. At the end of the day, it was me. If I try to be Kenny Malone, I can maybe copy a lick or whatever. The bottom line is that I'm not Kenny. I don't have his heartbeat. I'm just who I am. When I figured that out, I started playing better. At that point, I stopped playing drums and started playing music.

The minute you stop playing drums and start thinking musical—listening without an ego, hearing all the great things the other players are doing, and making decisions about how to highlight their ideas—you're doing something special.

What musical and personal attributes does a musician need to be successful?

There's a lot to it. It's more than just playing the drums or guitar. First of all, you have to be really honest with yourself. You have to know what your strengths and weaknesses are. You always have to work on your weaknesses. If you're not a fusion player, maybe you shouldn't take that gig.

You need to find out what you want to do with your music. There's a term called "music business." I knew at some point I wanted to be a drummer, but more importantly I wanted to *make a living.*

Passion is imperative. You have to have talent, but you have to have passion. That's what makes you work hard.

You need to assess what you want to do with your music. Do you want to be a professor, a touring musician, or a session player? You need to know. It's like this—where are you from?

I'm originally from Illinois.

I can go out on a Sunday drive without a map and drive around for a little while. I don't need a map for that. Now, if I'm trying to get to your house and haven't been there before, I had better have a map. I think everybody needs to have a plan for their career. I think it needs to be flexible. I don't think somebody should quit if they don't get exactly what they want.

I hate to say this, because I don't want to be negative. However, the music business is really different right now. You have to be very careful.

If I were just starting out right now, I would want to have some sort of degree to fall back on other than my playing.

I'd tell somebody to give themselves a certain number of years to complete a goal. It's not like the sixties, seventies, and eighties anymore. Record sales are in the toilet and CDs are probably on their way out. There's no middle class in the music industry anymore. There are the very successful types and the up-and-comers. Get a degree, take five years of your life, don't get married, and play every gig that comes your way. After each year, evaluate where you are in your career and decide if you're improving. Ask yourself who you are working with, what kind of money you're making, and be honest about where you are. If you haven't done anything in five years, are just hanging on from gig to gig, and can't afford a car or anything, you might want to think about another job.

I firmly believe that a young person should have an education, that they should not let anybody tell them that they can't be successful, but they should have a backup plan. Twenty years ago, I wouldn't say that.

Music is wonderful. There are people like myself that played sessions their whole career. I was blessed tremendously. There are people that just play on the weekends every now and again, and they have a wonderful time too. If you're going to make this your business, you need to treat it as a business. You need to do all the right things. Surround yourself with a lot of good people. Have a lot of irons in the fire. Be as versatile as possible. When that circle dries up, you'll have something else to do.

Like I said, if you're in a band, you might get a big record deal and never have to worry about money again. It happens, but rarely.

I never cared about being under one umbrella. I loved sessions because I got to work with so many people. I'd be with one group of people one day and an entirely different group the next. There's a lot of risk there. Not everybody is cut out for that. I didn't know if I was going to eat, but it was great when it started to happen. God gets the glory. I'm thankful.

These days, get an education, get a degree, and get something to fall back on. If you don't need it, great. If you have a dream, don't let anybody stop you.

Be smart about your career and know where you are and where you're going. If you dabble around for a lot of years, the next thing you know you're forty-five years old and too old to start a new career. I don't want to be negative, but that can happen.

My whole thing was about making a living. I didn't want to play just for the sake of playing. I can have as much fun playing thirty to forty minutes at the house as I can at a session, but I can't afford to do that. Chart your path and have a goal. Without that, you're just wandering.

That's worth its weight in gold. Thank you.

My pleasure. I enjoyed it.

3

KENNY MALONE

Kenny Malone's early musical training was as unique as his career. He was born in Colorado and studied at the Wells School of Music. Studying at the school gave him opportunities to perform with a sixteen-piece accordion band, accompany dance groups, play in an eighteen-piece marimba orchestra, and perform in any number of other situations that could be created with the available instrumentation. A career in the navy took him around the world performing with jazz big bands before heading the percussion department at the Navy School of Music. As head of the percussion department, he taught many percussionists using a curriculum he developed to expedite the learning process.

Malone moved to Nashville in 1970 and quickly established himself as a valuable addition to any rhythm section. While he was earning a good enough living to support a family, things really picked up for him after the world heard his contributions to the classic tunes "Drift Away" by Dobie Gray and "Amanda" by Don Williams. His creativity led him to use all manner of items (ashtrays, sticks, guitar bodies, countertops, spoons, pieces of metal) to achieve the sounds that would best accompany the likes of Johnny Cash, Waylon Jennings, Dolly Parton, Crystal Gayle, and Reba McEntire.

His inventiveness extends past the drum set, as he has developed his own method of hand drumming. His method and willingness to experiment defined the new grass style of percussion. It was practically a requirement to have Malone play on folk, acoustic, and new grass albums. He is a favorite of Béla Fleck, Alison Krauss, Alison Brown, Casey Driessen, and the many others that perform in that style. Constantly searching for the perfect sound, Malone has invented his own unique instruments to complement the plethora of situations in which he is invited to perform. He is still as in demand as ever to record and perform with top artists, a strong testimony of his keen ability to incorporate new ideas into a song.

In this interview, Malone gives a peek into his creative thought process, tells of lessons he's learned, and recounts many stories from the wide variety of artists he's had the opportunity to work with. As Tom Roady stated, "He is the least boring drummer you will ever hear in your life. I mean that with all the love and respect. I love him. He doesn't play like anyone else. Not just in Nashville but anywhere."

Where are you from originally?

Denver, Colorado. I banged on everything when I was a kid. I remember the day I decided I wanted to be a drummer was the day I heard Dixieland music. I think it was the Firehouse Five back in, like, 1943. My mom and dad got me a drum for Christmas. That started everything.

I studied at the Wells School of Music as a child. They had instructors on the third and fourth floors of this radio station that sponsored it. There was a music store downstairs. They had every kind of band you could imagine. My first band was a sixteen-piece accordion band. They taught big band and had full instrumentation. The other kids—like my sister, who was a dancer—would be included. There was a music and dance festival. It was a lot of the kids in Denver. I started there when I was nine or ten. They started me on marimba. I think I started playing drums when I turned ten. We played at prisons, air force bases, synagogues, everywhere. I played with an eighteen-piece marimba orchestra full of kids. The cathedrals really had a beautiful sound.

Who were the drummers that you looked up to at the time?

Oh, wow! My first idol was Gene Krupa. I saw Gene Krupa and Buddy Rich do a drum battle in Denver with Jazz at the Philharmonic with Ella Fitzgerald, Stan Getz, and all of these wonderful players. I was just hooked forever. That's what I wanted to do, and I did.

You spent some time in the navy.

I left Denver in 1956. I went in the navy. I went overseas in 1958 with my first big band. We had every chart you could think of. We'd practice all the time. It was a really hot band. Then I went to the big band in Washington, DC. We played for presidents and things. We played for John F. Kennedy. We went all over South America with Dwight Eisenhower in 1960.

We used to carry thirty or forty drumheads to sea. We had to stock our own because you couldn't find them overseas in those days. I got thrown in jail for breaking a drumhead in Naples, Italy. The man who owned the drum set didn't speak any English, I didn't speak any Italian, and he wanted to fight. The Italian police had one of my arms and the Shore Patrol grabbed the other arm to break up the fight. The Shore Patrol hauled me into headquarters, thank God. I was in jail all night long that night. I was restricted to the ship for three days after. I was trying to tell the guy that I could go back to my ship to get him another head, but he couldn't understand me.

The same thing happened in Izmur, Turkey, a few months later. We were in a club, and I broke a head in the middle of a song. I said, "Denny, as soon as the song's over, grab your hat because I just broke a head. I'll meet you down at the fleet landing." The song's over. Bang! Everybody's applauding and the band ran right out the front door single file [laughs]. We're down at the fleet landing dressed up in dress whites. Our full commander came running down all out of breath. He's yelling, "Hey! Some drummer just broke a drumhead." I was the drummer, so I walked up to him and explained what happened in Naples. He said, "Aw yeah. Take the admiral's barge, get him a new head, come back, and give it to him. So we got an extra hour and a half of liberty that time [laughs]. You learn how to work the system, you know?

There was a plane crash that year that killed all of my buddies. It was a midair plane collision. I was sick and didn't make the flight. I slept out on the deck in Buenos Aires because it was so hot on our ship. Mosquitoes ate me alive and I swelled up real bad. I went to the lieutenant and asked to stay back. The head drummer got on the plane. That changed my life big time. That's when I transferred to the school.

I became the head of the percussion department at the Navy School of Music. I had around forty students per week, including students from the army, navy, and marines. We had to find shortcuts for them as teachers so they could be ready in six months. That's how long the Navy School of Music lasted. That was its former name. Now it's just the School of Music. We had to teach them big band and combo playing, how to play dances. You know, all of the practical things they need when they go overseas and play all of these different places. I have the manual that I wrote on my website.

So the first shortcut to helping was using the Jim Chapin book, *Advanced Techniques for the Modern Drummer*. Instead of starting them on page one, which is hand independence, we started on page thirty-five. We only used the first three exercises on that page because all of the other figures are just variations on those. We'd show them how to practice really slow and to count as part of their sound. We made sure they got a real good grasp of "the dance" before they went faster, and they all got it. By that, I mean anybody who applied himself.

The next thing that we did was take two pages out of Ralph C. Pace's book. He had a wonderful book called *Variations of Drumming*. There were long and short notes. We'd take two pages out of that and play long notes on the kick drum and short notes on the snare drum while superimposing a ride cymbal pattern over the top. That got their four-way coordination happening. They could go out *that day* and practice with a seventeen-piece big band. There were five of them going every period. It was a *big thing*, man!

What made you decide to move to Nashville?

I didn't want to raise my kids in New York, Miami, or Chicago. I had heard a lot of bad things about the big cities. I thought Nashville was kind of a small town. I figured there were a few main streets with a few studios. I didn't know anything about the city [laughs].

I could really play when I got here [Nashville]. We got to play with this wonderful faculty-led big band once a year in the navy. We'd have guest artists sit in with us, like Frank Rosolino, Clark Terry, Doc Severinsen, and all these other big stars. It would be an All-Regional Band Instrumental clinic for band directors. So I was playing with that group once a year. That's all I was playing. The rest of the time I was teaching, doing administration, ordering fifty-three navy drum sets for the fleet.

When I came to Nashville, I had fast chops, I could kick a big band, and I could read anything. I remember one of my first sessions—my God—I was working for this guy, Bob Montgomery, who used to produce Bobby Goldsboro in the early 1970s. We were playing a bluegrass-type thing, and I thought, "I think a Montuno beat might work on this" [laughs]. He stopped the band and said, "What are you doing back there?" Those were his exact words. He says, "I don't need any cymbals on this. All I need is a kick drum and a backbeat. That's all I need. You can pack up your cymbals because I don't need them."

From that moment, I really started hearing each note before, during, and after, and how they led to each other as part of a complete word or sentence. Instead of notes, now, it had transformed me to trying to get the perfection of just that one single beat—the low-high relationship. How do you keep perfect time and form your own metronome inside your body? I learned ways to do that. It involves different functions, like breathing, feeling, counting . . . giving a note its length and making that part of the note. Instead of "bam," it can be "baaaaaaam." It can be as long as you want it.

I never heard the lyrics to a song before I got to Nashville in 1970. I never paid any attention. I always treated the human voice as another instrument that could change sibilants, but I didn't pay attention. I could usually pick out the title line of the song, but not much more.

Do you think you were overplaying when you moved here?

Yeah, not for very long, though [laughs]. That changed quickly, transferring simplicity to every single song where you could really see how these things were formed in time. It gave me time to use my imagination. We used to do jingles with no click tracks. There weren't any. It was in the early 1970s. They still weren't around much in the mid-1970s, but it didn't matter. The arrangers would write the song or jingle. If it was over time, they'd take out a measure. It's funny. If it was just a little over time, the band could literally think themselves into the perfect time. We'd play it a certain tempo, they'd say that we needed to shave a second and a half off over the course of sixty seconds, and we'd do it! Time and time again! Once you get the right notes and *dance* going, you can just think yourself right into that pocket.

That's how I count off songs. When I went on the road with Crystal Gayle, there were some good times there.

How did you meet people when you got to Nashville?

The only name I had was Ron Oates. He's a friend of mine and a piano player. He was doing sessions about that time. I had taken a three-day leave from the navy to come down and see Nashville. He took me around to a session or something. When I got out of the navy, we were staying at a motel called the Alamo Plaza with four kids, a dog, and one bedroom, man. Coming here was rough. My radiator blew up ten miles out of Norfolk, Virginia. It was one of those trips [laughs]. We went through our savings in about ninety days. I had ninety days to make up my mind whether I wanted to leave the navy or return with my same rank.

On the eighty-ninth day, I wasn't working enough to support a family. I called one of my buddies named Bill Humble, and then he called a few of his buddies. From that, I got a few country club gigs, and it eased the financial strain. That really helped me.

I got in with a great rhythm section. Bobby Dyson was the leader of the group. He was the bass player. Ron Oates was in the group, of course. Jim Colvard was on electric guitar. He was a wild man. Curly

Chalker played steel guitar, and Bobby Thompson was on rhythm guitar. They were doing a lot of sessions at the time. When I showed up, it was like "bang!" I did one demo and ended up doing a lot after that. Shortly after, we did Carl Perkins's record, which was my first master session.

I did a few more sessions, and then Mentor Williams brought Dobie Gray in for "Drift Away." That became really big at the same time that "Amanda" did, which was the B-side of "Come Early Morning" on Don Williams's album. That was his first record, and it did pretty well. "Amanda" became the hit, though. It just took off. This was in 1973. After that, I had three or four sessions every day. It was a fast pace then. We had an hour between sessions.

What was the "Drift Away" session like? Was it laid back?

Oh, yeah, those cats . . . whew. Reggie Young, David Briggs, and all of them. It was a great sound and great-sounding studio. The engineer was Gene Eichelberger. It was like a pentagon-shaped drum booth. I got a great sound in there, especially if I hit them hard. That wasn't hard to do [laughs]. I used a deep snare on that song for the first time. It was a field drum. An inexpensive, wooden rim, mahogany shell field drum that was ten inches deep. That's how I got that big boom! That changed a few things right there.

Those were some good sessions.

What happened when you pulled out a ten-inch-deep snare drum?

They didn't care! They were all for it! They were crazy, man. It was after it came out on the radio when using that kind of drum became a norm. People really wanted that sound.

I remember "Loving Arms" and all of those great records with Dobie. We did three or four, and the last we did was "Watch Out for Lucy." We went out to Los Angeles to kick it off at the Troubadour. It was a fight night, man. There were three fights in the audience before we even started. There was a fight right in the front row. It was so packed nobody could move. There was a fight out of the back door, and a guy fell out of the balcony and broke his shoulder. In "Watch Out for Lucy," there was a line that says, "Because every Saturday night she likes to get out and ball." They debated whether or not to use that track for a long time before we recorded it. Back then it was really taboo to say things like that. Now, it's nothing. No DJs would play the song. That's the last thing we ever did.

Wow!

I know it! Watch out for Lucy [laughs]!

There's a lot of sound going on in "Drift Away." Was somebody playing percussion?

No. I added that woodblock later.

The snare drum was different. Was there anything special about your kit at the time?

I was using double heads. That wasn't always the case back then. They sounded great. He got a great, full sound. Back then, on tape, it sounded amazing. My daughter sent me a copy on a CD, but the low end doesn't feel like it's there.

When I got here, the studio drums were what we were expected to use. They sounded bad, man. I wanted a different sound, so I started using my own drums and learning how to get a sound. I had to go through the full education. You literally have to become a recording engineer to a certain degree to know how to talk to one. It's important to be able to speak intelligently about what you need to hear in the headphones, for example. Acoustics, whew. That's what has kept me interested all of these years. The "why does it do that?" kind of thing. It's like every spot you sit in a room changes your sound—especially with drums and low frequencies. I can put them in some spots, and the low frequencies will completely disappear. Sometimes it's a foot or so because of the standing waves and stuff. It's a whole education.

It was a lot different back then. All of the artists used to sing live. There was no overdubbing. There might be a word or two to fix, but it was pretty much top to bottom singing. I got here right when sixteen-track first came in. They had a three-track recorder over at Columbia. All of those artists at Columbia were all live. That was my education on leakage. Why does leakage make my drums sound bad to me? Why don't they have any "smack"?

I had to go through all of the different technology changes. I did the first computer recordings here with Rick Powell. That was over at his place. I forget where it was. He did mostly Christian music. He had a computer that he had to get on a ladder to patch things in. We cut all these gospel groups in the late 1970s. It was some time around there.

I did the first direct-to-disc over at Soundstage Studios. We ran the cables across the alley into Masterfonics. We could save one generation of tape noise by doing it that way. They cut the record at the same time you were playing. It was a big band too. There were some hard charts because there were some really great jazz players who wrote these great charts in town. I made the mistake of pulling two songs of sheet music off of the music stand at the same time. We were halfway through the album. You have to start the whole record over if you mess up. There's only ten seconds between when a song ends and the next one begins, so you have to be ready to go. Bang! It was an interesting challenge and great in those days.

I did the first digital recording over at Woodland Studios. I think it had Farrell Morris on percussion. It was a small band. I remember then that it wasn't the same. The sound literally made the cymbals sound like glass. It was more of a *tsssssss*—real false with no transients. That was right at the time where the Japanese, I believe, were supplying all of the major radio stations with digital technology. We had to get used to it because that became the norm. It's like MP3s to people now. Most people don't care because that sound is comfortable for them now.

I came up in the high-fidelity days.

You had a lot of guys who looked out for you at first.

I think the first session was over at Cedarwood. I was so nervous that I didn't hear a note I played. It seemed like everything was a mistake. We'd get ready to do a song, and I'd just have the intro written and they were ready to do the song. I didn't know anything about their charts and stuff. I knew how to write music, but not the Nashville Number System. Somehow I made it through, and they asked me to work with them that night and the next morning. We were doing all different styles—some were Latin and such. That's what started it.

What were some of the other places you were working?

DBM Studios was where the producer said, "What are you doing?" Oh, Jack Clement's place. That's "Cowboy" Jack Clement. I've known him the entire time I've been here. We would work out at his place, which is now the Sound Emporium. Of course, I worked at Studios A and B a lot. That's where Don Williams cut all of his records. There were a lot of people that used those rooms.

Donna Fargo recorded "The Happiest Girl in the Whole USA" there. That was a big song. Cowboy bought Jack's Tracks, which became Allen Reynolds's place, who produced Garth Brooks. In fact, Garth actually owns it now and named it Allentown. I worked at Columbia a lot. They used to record big orchestras live in Columbia A and in RCA Room A. All of the big studios were happening then. They had multistudios. Wow, there were a lot of studios even back then, and I thought there were two main streets before I got here.

Which drums were you using?

I built them. That was after I had everything stolen. The first kit I had was an old Gretsch that I refinished and painted. I got with Sonor after I did "Drift Away." They were wonderful drums because I liked the maple-wood sound. Then I got with Pearl because I could never get parts for Sonor drums back then. I had a Pearl fiberglass and wood combination drum set. I didn't really care for it. I could never get rid of the glass sound. I was glad those drums were stolen. That's when I started building my own. That led to everything.

How did they get stolen?

They were in my driveway. It snowed and I didn't want to take them inside. Some guy cleaned them out.

When was that?

Probably in the mid-1970s. When I went to the factory to get some new drums, I saw some raw shells and thought, "Now's the time." It only took about two weeks to build a whole set. Cavalier Vans painted them the same color that I have now, which is about the galaxies and stuff.

Are you a Pearl artist?

No, I don't advertise for anybody anymore. I always like to use my own inventions and things. I made those drums, and they were edged opposite from the way Pearl did it at that time. I always had to explain what I wanted. I was doing some clinic and things and didn't want to deal with it anymore. I just use my own stuff.

What are some of the instruments that you have made?

I have some cajónes and a shaka that I made. They're smaller cajónes. They were tuned when I finally heard them for the first time. It was a D, a D octave lower, and a B down below that. They were great for bluegrass because they are usually in D and G. I used eighth-inch plywood for heads. I wanted to see how small and large I could build something. I was going to make one even bigger, but I would have had to squash the angle ten degrees because it couldn't fit through doorways. The one I envisioned would have a four-feet-square head, but it couldn't have a long barrel so it could be turned on its side to play.

[Malone plays his trapezoidal wooden drum creation nicknamed "The Beast."]

Do you hear all of those sounds? I put these spokes on top to re-create the sound of the wind blowing or water rushing. It's really fun to play. They're made out of hickory like drumsticks. It's really strong wood. I added these beads on wire for a *ts, ts* sound.

Playing from one end of the drum to the other gives me a range of low–high log sounds [demonstrates]. I made this because I was trying to see how many different sizes of cajónes I could make. Eric Darken gave me a cajón, and I wanted to see if I could get a bigger size. So Sam Bacco, that crazy nut who's a good friend of mine—he and I build drums together—was trying to figure out the perfect mathematical size to build the best one according to the Fibonacci series. We thought the proportions and the angles would be great. It came out to ten degrees. The problem was that it was too long when we finished it and there were no low frequencies. I started cutting it down just to see what would happen.

The box is made out of half-inch birch plywood. The end is five-thirty-seconds-inch door skin that I bought at Lowe's. This little door at the bottom lowers the pitch when I close it. I've been meaning to add a foot pedal that will close it, but I haven't gotten around to it. I call it the Beast because the plural of *cajón* is *cajónes*. I'd rather not have to explain that to everybody all the time with them snickering. A friend named it the Beast, and it's been that ever since. I do think it looks like a wildebeest. It's got the spokes like a mane [laughs].

[Malone points to a drum shaped like a seashell referred to as the "conch-a-drum."]

Now with this one, I had a dream when I was forty years old about an old man playing seashells like drums. They were arranged like a xylophone or marimba. The seashells were like clamshells, and he was playing them with bamboo reeds in my dream. I got to wondering how that would really sound. So I went to the ocean and started collecting seashells to experiment with.

I then took a class over at Centennial Arts Center with Lena Lucas. I *knew* it was possible to get a seashell drum. The first drum I made was like a doumbek. You have to make a ridge around it to create an opposing rim to seat a head. That let me use regular tension rods. We had to mill these rods [on the conch-a-drum] out of solid brass, and Sam Bacco put these rims on here. It worked perfectly. It's tunable. We tucked it like a conga skin, so it's really easy on the hands [Malone plays the drum]. This is just made out of clay coils. I put it on a turntable. I learned how to wedge the clay, add grog—this is, Raku with a lot of grog—so it wouldn't shrink so much. When clay is fired, it shrinks 12 to 15 percent, so it has to have structural integrity with compression. You have to roll out these coils that are about as big around as my little finger, make it perfectly round, compress the clay, and add another coil at a time. This got tricky because I had to make a spiral because that's what a conch shell does. I had to build bridges and things to keep it sturdy all the way up. The whole thing was a half-inch thick before it was fired. I based this shell off of one my daughter gave me. I love building stuff and finding the sound.

I didn't bring the heavy one that I made. I got a hernia from it one time [laughs]. I did! I was running into the Arts & Sciences Museum down there—the kids place. It weighs fifty-nine pounds. I was running because it was really hot outside, and I felt the hernia go. I had to get that fixed.

I had an idea to put multiple drumheads on one chamber. I didn't care what shape it was. I envisioned kind of a sweet potato shape in my mind. I got it done! It has two heads. One of the heads wraps around the drum. It has its own hardware, so it's tunable. The rim is made out of falcon wood, which is really hard. I have a picture of it on my website. I call it the Og. It also has a knee port on the side that lets me lower the tone. It has a chin hole that I can use to bend the tone. I wanted to construct a rawhide braided cable to an arc that let me sit inside a big C that would let it hang down. I wanted all of the actions to come toward my body instead of away, but it looked like a big ham hanging there [laughs]. Sam Bacco gave me an old trampoline frame. It would have been so simple and practical to set inside a stand and play.

I made a foot drum one time that I could play with my feet to get that low–high. My first idea was to make this thing that looked like a squashed balloon with a nozzle coming off the front. Sam Bacco gave me this thick mule head, and I was going to use that. There wasn't any sound because that wave has to come out the bottom for the low end. Live and learn, I guess.

Have you changed how you build equipment over the years?

Yeah! This brush system I have on my djembe is something that was cool. I knew it needed that sound when I got it. I built a bracket and put a brush on the side. I can use my hand and fingers. One of these days I'm going to get a drawing and put it on my website. It's easy to make, and it works. I use it on everything. I use that bracket a lot on the road with a snare, this djembe, and a sixteen-inch cymbal. The snare and cymbal go in a suitcase, and the djembe and stand go in another case so I can fly with it.

Who do you use that set up with?

Darrell Scott. We just did a thing at TPAC [Tennessee Performing Arts Center] called Jammin' at Hippie Jacks. It was two sets of *magic*. It's the only time I believe that I've ever captured that magic and it played us. You can see it. They got it on video.

I saw a video or two of that while I was researching for this interview.

Man, he is such an artist. That's what I'm talking about. You *have* to believe him when you listen to him. When he does a song, he presents it where it inspires you to play to the intensity of those words that are happening at the moment. That's the magic when it plays us. I just enjoy the ride.

Did you ever make a piccolo snare drum to match the trend?

I remember that phase. That's part of a sound that we can tune to. All you have to do to get a piccolo sound is turn your snare drum over. I've built piccolo drums before, and I like them for playing with my fingers and effect stuff. You can't get it to project past the front of the stage without hitting it too hard.

You have to make sure to craft a good snare bed into the drum. When the snares lay flat across the drum, they don't leave the drum when you hit it too hard. You can get real sensitive to where your drum doesn't sound like *pung, pung*. That's when you know the snare wires are too tight.

You mentioned that you like to listen to lyrics to guide your performance. What sort of head space did Dobie Gray's voice put you in while recording that song?

I live the song. I live the lyrics. That's what I do all the time. That's what transformed my focus from playing just with the instruments to hearing the lyrics. Literally, I try to live the emotions of the song. I always want to know what the lyrics are. If there are words to it, I want to see them, hear them, and know what they're about. When does it get sad? I need to be able to respond to it right then to paint the right picture. That's what makes the difference in "hit music," if you want to call it that. It's special because you're just hanging on, man. The song passes through you, and you're just responding to the overall thing.

Every sound that is going on at the moment, whew, without preplanning, is what matters to me. Those sessions where everything is planned out is like painting by numbers to me. That's why I quit doing sessions one time. I'd had it. Everything I was playing sounded the same.

When was that?

It was in the late 1970s, when I went on the road with Crystal Gayle. It may have been in the early 1980s. I just gave away my answering machine. I didn't do many sessions for ten years!

We played down at Captain Hornblower's Jazz Club in Key West with Charles Cochran and Joe Allen. That was the group that we first started in Nashville. We played down at Roger Miller's King of the Road every Sunday night for a year. They started broadcasting it live. Musicians started hanging out and jamming with us. That's how I met some people. We went to Key West, and Crystal Gayle came and sang with us one evening from Miami. We became her rhythm section and toured for a year. We had done some records with her like "Brown Eyes Blue," but I wasn't playing live. It literally changed my whole life, when I started getting a good balance between recording and live playing. The instant response of the audience—they're part of it. It gives a song a reason to be. It's for listeners. I still have to play live, and I do. There are some special things now.

We talked about Gene Krupa. Who were you listening to when you got to Nashville?

What really got me to move here was that I really loved jazz and big band jazz, but I heard Blood, Sweat, and Tears. I said, "That's it. Fourteen years, and I'm out of here [the navy]." It had that nice flavor to it. Them, Chicago, and other bands of that style. When I came here, Blood, Sweat, and Tears were just wonderful. I saw them at the Belcourt recently. I had to leave because they were so loud I had my fingers in my ears. I was sitting in the back row, and they were wonderful! I don't know if they had earplugs or what. I couldn't stand the volume and had to leave after four songs. They were great. I wanted to stay. They had two drummers.

I was always into big band jazz. I liked Stan Kenton. I heard all of the big bands when I was a kid. I loved Tommy and Jimmy Dorsey.

Was it easy to translate that to how people were playing here?

Yeah. I'm really thankful for that education because that really is the basis for how I play everything. I really enjoy the "we can let go of the rules" kind of playing and allow the song to play me.

There's a low–high relationship, tone, and how we relate to it in Western music. It's all like a march.

Can you explain that concept?

All of our Western music stems from the drum and fife days: the statements and answers of music. Our cadences [Kenny sings while tapping his foot] are shown in fig. 3.1. You can sing me any song, and I can play that cadence to it. Think about that drum rhythm that comes with every little keyboard [Kenny sings], shown in fig. 3.2. It might be voiced another way, or slower or faster, but that's on everything. It's like a statement and an answer [Kenny sings] shown in fig. 3.3 is the statement that's answered by fig. 3.4. I feel like that's just like the statement and answer of the cadence, in fig. 3.5, which gets answered in the same way by fig. 3.6.

Figure 3.1

Figure 3.2

Figure 3.3

Figure 3.4

Figure 3.5

Figure 3.6

Any rock song that you hear with the I–IV–V progression is all from some kind of a march, and that's a dance. It translates because it's a universal language.

It's a fact that we create our musical "home" before we're, like, four years old. We form all the harmonic relationships of our culture's music, which becomes our comfort zone for the rest of our life. People in India will feel their comfort zone, their music, and their phrase all of their life. That's the music we gravitate toward.

The snare drum itself comes from the drum and the fife. The only reason they added snares was to get that *bick, bick, bick* to be heard over a battle to send orders. I would have *hated* to be a drummer back then. They didn't even have a gun! They're charging into the line . . . are you kidding me? See you guys later [laughs]!

I would have been good for nothing out there.

God almighty! I know!

When you listen to another drummer, what do you listen for?

How he's fitting with the music. What's the song about and if he's playing something that adds or detracts from the song. There's always rhythm, melody, and harmony. That's the order they taught us in the navy. Rhythm was the most important part of music. Melody was the second most important, and harmony was the third. Most of our music today has our harmony saturated. Every strong beat or phrase has harmony, harmony, harmony, harmony. It isn't like that in other cultures, like in India. Melodic lines might cross and form harmony, but they don't go at it for harmony.

I listen to how a drummer is fitting with a song or band. Is he part of the band or just crashing and banging through everything? That's a lot of it. That's youth. When I was young, I couldn't play soft. My dad used to come in, throw the newspaper down, and yell, "Can't you play those softer?" You can't at that age. I was like fourteen or fifteen. I had to buy my own drum set with milk and newspaper routes. I appreciated them. I broke three drum heads the first day I got them. That was before plastic!

You've played on a lot of records over the years. You've also had your own bands like Tone Patrol.

Oh, yeah! That was a fun band! That was Dave Pomeroy, Larry Chaney, Biff Watson, Sam Bacco, and me. We wanted to play. We wrote our own stuff and jammed. It was a wonderful band. We played for a year at Douglas Corner and recorded every night we played. Dave edited all those tracks. He took all the songs we wrote out and just used the jams that we launched from the songs. It's like a forty-five-minute, continuous . . . *wild* thing!

We've got a new band going now. It's the same thing, man. I wanted to play and they wanted to play. It's Jonathan Yudkin on violin; Pat Bergeson on jazz guitar, acoustic guitar, and harmonica; and Dave Pomeroy on upright and electric bass. We're just learning our repertoire right now. We want to play things that are fun to play, like some of those old standards with the great melodies. The first song we worked on was "Charade." It's the most unique treatment of the song. It's beautiful.

Do you have a band name?

I wanted to call it Three Musicians and a Drummer, but I don't think they want to call it that [laughs].

Let's talk about how you started playing hand drums.

When I first started playing with Don Williams, I would play the basic *boom, chick, boom, chick*, low, high, low, high. After we did the track, I'd overdub a conga drum and do the attack like *book, bik, book, bik*. You can play melodies with that muffled sound. You can actually follow the bass guitar or go in contrary motion. There a lot of possibilities. It puts the attack on the bass guitar that the tic-tac bassists used to do on a lot of country songs. Somebody would take an electric guitar, roll all the bottom frequencies out, use a pick, and play the notes really short with the upright bass. It added that *bik* sound to the bass. Those are the most important frequencies to me in keeping time—three kHz and ten kHz. That's right around where the attack on the kick and hi-hat are. I think that's why they started calling it a "kick" drum because of that *kik, kik* attack.

When you started using your hands on the drum set, how was that received?

After we made a couple of hit records, like with Don Williams, they didn't question it anymore. Some people didn't want an African drum on a country song. It was different back then. If you play it right, it doesn't have to sound like something African. You're after a sound rather than a culture. All of the sound changes are there like on any drum.

The Nashville drumming community is such a brotherhood. I know Larrie Londin had a drum shop. Did you spend time there?

It was fun! Larrie and I had a ball. He was such a generous cat. He'd come out of a studio and see me carrying my drums. He'd say, "Why don't you grow up and get cartage?" Or he'd slam a pedal into me and say, "Here! You like this pedal? It's yours." We were always really close.

I got to teach Larrie a couple of ways to kick a big band using those short cuts from the navy I told you about. He always credited me with teaching him how to read. He already knew how to read. He just didn't know how to apply it like long, short, with a big band. With those few times we got together, it dawned on him. He started playing with a big band and just had a blast!

I hated to see him go, man.

His place was called D.O.G.

Oh, man! When my drums were stolen, I ran over there. Debbie, his wife, said, "Here. Use one of Larrie's sets, and I'll send over a couple of technicians to help set it up. I only had a half hour, and we made the session. It was fast! After he loaned me a set for a couple of weeks, plus cymbals, and after I got my drums done, he called me and sang "Happy Birthday." I said, "It isn't my birthday." He said, "Yes it is. Happy birthday! Those cymbals are yours." He was always giving me stuff. What a nut!

Who were some of the other guys hanging around at the time?

Jerry Carrigan and Kenny Buttrey. Kenny was on top of the new, 1970s approach with Area Code 615. That group had Wayne Moss, Charlie McCoy, David Briggs, and those guys. That band became Barefoot Jerry, which I joined later right off the bat. It started to look too much like it wanted to go on the road, so I stopped. I didn't want to do that, man.

When I got here, there were about five drummers doing most of the work. There was Buddy Harman, Karl Himmel, Willie Ackerman—Willie did all of the Opry stuff. When he first started, they used to hide his snare drum behind a hay bale. I thought that was amazing. They didn't want to show drums on *The Grand Ole Opry*. He also did all of the *Hee Haw* stuff. He let Hargus "Pig" Robbins drive his car one night. Pig's blind, you know. He played a great piano. We did a thousand records together over the years. I think he drove down the street in Willie's car, and Willie was giving him verbal instructions. That was a wild night [laughs]!

It is amazing that you have had such a long career. How have you seen the playing change? You're obviously a great musician—that's always relevant—but what conscious decisions have you made?

Well, when things got slow the first time the industry crashed, when the Exit/In closed all those years ago, there seemed like nothing was going on. We started playing at the Bluebird Cafe to get some kind of action going where people would go out and see something. There weren't any clubs going that I knew about. That did generate some action. I started building drums at that time. I mean, really building, which is something I've always wanted to do. That took my time and energy. It was a positive new direction.

It was like, I played this drum (seashell) with Johnny Cash and the Carter Family at Cowboy's studio. Cowboy looked at it for a long time and said, "Kenny, all I want to know is—is that thing going to attack me?" Johnny was a funny cat [laughs].

Johnny Cash was great. He used to smoke. He and Joe Allen were in a rental car going across Canada. Johnny was leaned back in the passenger seat. Joe said, "Johnny, crack that window, will ya?" Johnny took his boot and kicked the windshield. He put a big crack in it. That's what Joe asked for. He cracked the window [laughs].

You obviously have the kind of credibility that allows you to make suggestions that might get a sideways glance from other guys. Do you ever have to censor yourself for different scenarios?

It's hard to shut off the critic in yourself, but I don't think about it anymore. If it is too far, the song will show me. If I'm playing something that doesn't work, it literally shows me. People change what we're doing as we're going along and developing a song. The words need to be believable with the presentation (the rest of the arrangement). The artists that I like to play with, and usually do, are guys like Darrell Scott and Tim O'Brien—all of these wonderful songwriters and players that can present the song and it's true. It's believable at the moment no matter what environment you're in. It's like a play on a stage and they're the lead actor. They present those words that just feel right. Not everybody can do that. It's hard to transform yourself, especially if you're having a rotten day or something. It's tough to sing this happy song when you're in the dumps. They live the song, and that's my thing. That makes things right.

What does an upbeat, happy song bring out of you?

I try to bring my emotions to match that intensity. I try to think of the kind of happy. Is it thankful? Frolicking? What flavor is it? I imagine dancers in my mind and how they would dance to it. That helps me a lot. You don't even have to see people in your mind. All you have to see is forms creating the dance. What am I imagining? How do they move to this song? It'll show you what to play.

How much of an influence did your sister have on you as a dancer?

Yeah. She was into ballet and aerial acrobatics. She did aerial acrobats until she missed and landed on her head. She had amnesia for three days and gave up dancing and acrobatics. I grew up playing for the Denver Ballet and all different kinds of shows all around the city. I was exposed to how they move and communicate. I just finished playing with the Nashville Ballet. Man, they are world class. Let me tell you. They are unbelievable. This time I knew the songs well enough that I could look at the dancers. It's nice to do that so you don't hit a big *boom* when the graceful ballerina is hitting the stage. You can tailor to the show [laughs]. You don't want "Swan Lake" to come across the stage with the stripper floor tom beat [laughs]. They choreographed three of Darrell Scott's songs and three of Guy Clark's songs. Guy is a case, man. We've been together since I can remember. He writes some great songs.

Darrell Scott is some of your favorite work. Do you have any others that you listen to like that?

Oh, yeah. The first time I recorded with Béla Fleck. He came in, I had my drums set up, and he said, "Why don't you give me about three minutes of a drum solo? I'll come in and join you." And he did. That's how we started his album *Deviation*. I was using brushes and stuff.

Had you met him before that?

No [laughs].

Those were his first words to you?

Yeah!

Wow!

We had a jazz group together. It was his groups called Banjo Jazz. We'd experiment with some sounds and everything. We went to Washington, DC, and did a show up there and in Baltimore at Ethel Ennis's jazz club. It was me, Béla, Tom Roady was playing percussion, Kirby Shelstad on vibraphone, and Mark Schatz on bass. We had a blast. That was just before the Wootens and the others.

You were on the cutting edge of the new grass sound.

Yeah, and, like were we talking about, that was before isolation. They used to set new grass up in a circle at Lee Hazen's Studio by the Pond. We shared overhead microphones. I just used one drum or whatever. They'd record the whole thing. That's how it was then.

How was the energy? Did you know that you were doing something really new and cool?

Yeah! It was different! It wasn't just drum set stuff. You were getting the sound of the song. We made that work first. I'm always trying to get down to the essence of a song. It's always a challenge. I try to get it as simple as can be and move on from there. The low–high has become so important, where I put those, and what frequencies they are. What will work with the vocal and getting out of their range. Don Williams used to have a real low voice. I couldn't use a deep snare. That sound was in his way. I had to tune it the right way to get out of his way. It was a funky sound, man, on "Tulsa Time" and all of that.

I did some work with Alison Brown, and they spoke very highly of you. What were those records like?

Oh, man! That's magic stuff right there, too. Alison has the most beautiful sound. She has a unique sound on her banjo to me. They let me go where I wanted to go. They let the song evolve. It's so much fun. I can find the "true" sounds. I don't usually set up a whole set. I might put up a basic set, but it's constantly changing and growing until that sound happens. Then *bang*! It's there. Boy, she plays some wonderfully unique stuff.

I did a concert with them at a Japanese Cherry Blossom special. It was so cool. It was unique, different, and some difficult charts. Writing those out and seeing the time signature changes was great. I loved doing that. She fits melodies in so well around shifting meters.

Looking at folk, country, and new grass, what types of considerations do you bring to each of those? Or do you change your approach?

Usually the people that I work for let me play what I feel. There are no preconceptions. Sometimes I'll give them some choices, and they know right away. I always try to find out the flavor that they want or if there are any questions about what they want. When I hear a song being performed for the first time, the first thing I try to think about is how I feel like dancing to it. That's all you have to do, man, is remember the dance. You've got the time, so you can do whatever you want to do. Whenever you count the song off, the dance is there. You know where it is because that's the flavor.

Each style has its own dance.

Yeah.

You mentioned Farrell Morris, Tom Roady, and Sam Bacco, who are three percussionists in town. I'm not sure a whole lot has been written about Farrell.

We did a lot of sessions together. He did about everything percussion-wise there is. He worked with orchestras, small groups, and everything. He was a trendsetter. He had equipment you couldn't even imagine. He had so much. I always used to tease him. We were at Compass Records studio, which was the Glaser brothers' studio [Glaser Sound Studios]. The studio is on the second floor, and there isn't an elevator. After we finished a song, the producer asked, "Does anybody hear anything else on this?" I said, "Yeah, timpani" [laughs]. Farrell would give me a look like, "Thanks, buddy."

Who were the guys that were hiring Farrell? We know that it was difficult getting drums on some country records.

It was like that. Charlie McCoy was another utility guy. He could play anything—trumpet, harmonica, or whatever. He could do a little of this and a little of that. They used to do it live back then too.

He had some freedom to put stuff together. It was pretty easygoing once it got going. He would work with anybody. He would be there no matter what you'd play. He was a true artist, like Sam Bacco is. Tom Roady, geez, he can do anything. That first jazz thing with Béla, Tom, and me was great.

Can you compare Tom Roady and Farrell Morris?

They have two different styles. I don't know. I can hear it, but I can't describe it. It's an attitude in how they play an instrument like congas. Tom plays them differently than Farrell. They're both right, but different. After you get that good, it's all subjective. There's a half dozen guys that are geniuses for every instrument in this town. It's unbelievable how this town is such a center for great musicians! There is magic here. It's amazing how many times a group plays through a song for the first time and it's perfect. They don't miss. How lucky can I be to play with people like that?

How did your DVD come about?

It was a result of playing with Tim O'Brien in Pagosa Spring, Colorado. All of the artists had to do a workshop. It was on a mountainside.

There were about thirty people that came up to me. A seven-year-old came up to me. He couldn't sit still. I was able to show him some things. If I would have had the DVD, he could have taken it home. I made it for beginners that maybe have never played, or accomplished drummers that want a new way to look at things. It took over five years to make. I was very happy to have some people that believed in me. I'm very proud of it. It's called *Drumming with Your Hands*. It's on my website—kennymalone.net—or at Fork's Drum Shop.

In closing, what are some of the critical musical attributes that you feel a musician needs to be successful?

Attitude. That's sounds simple, but it isn't. When you walk into a studio here, everybody knows you can play. You don't ever go into a studio and there isn't somebody who can't deliver. At least, I don't see that. If you can have fun with people and get the job done, and they can have fun with you, they are the ones that hire you. Not the producers. Not the record companies. It's the fellow musicians. When a producer asks somebody who to get, they're going to say a name because they're good to work with. That's how you develop a network of friends and people that you can work with. That's the most important part of it. That, being on time, and being sober.

Knowing as many varieties of music is important. Play with everybody you can play with in all different styles. They're going to show you something. It will also force you to make it work in the moment. I don't care what style it is. If it works, people will play off and with each other. That kind of contact will take you into a different spot. You won't even remember what you played because it's all so natural.

You've got to be musically humble. That's listening with big ears. You've got to listen to everything at once versus staying in your own little world. Hear the whole band *now*. That will tell you where to put that next note.

4

TOM ROADY

Tom Roady (January 17, 1949–November 27, 2011) grew up in the St. Louis metropolitan area and began to refine his craft in local recording studios and by playing in local bands. His first break came when he earned a gig with Phil Driscoll in 1971. He met many musicians through that experience and was able to establish himself as a session musician in St. Louis; Memphis, Tennessee; and the musical hotbed of Muscle Shoals, Alabama, with the legendary Muscle Shoals Sound Rhythm Section.

According to Roady, he learned the musical lessons that would become the hallmarks of his playing while recording with drummer Roger Hawkins (of the Muscle Shoals Sound Rhythm Section) on a nearly daily basis. His time in Muscle Shoals afforded him opportunities to record with artists such as Art Garfunkel, Paul Simon, Percy Sledge, and the Staple Singers while continuously building a unique instrument inventory.

His career would continue to diversify as his reputation grew. Opportunities in the music industry made him an in-demand percussionist in Los Angeles, Miami, Muscle Shoals, Nashville, and Memphis. Roady was able to adapt to the stylistic nuances of the disco, R&B, and pop albums he was recording throughout that period.

He moved to Nashville in 1982 and quickly began working with one of the hottest local bands, the Nerve. It wasn't long before he was an in-demand percussionist in the recording studios. Roady's ability to enhance a song can be heard on many of the biggest albums of the 1980s to 2000s. His work with artists like Suzy Bogguss, the Dixie Chicks, Vince Gill, Trisha Yearwood, and Wynonna Judd pushed the realm of possibility for percussion on country records.

Tom Roady passed away in his sleep on November 27, 2011, while traveling to a performance with Ricky Skaggs in Clemson, South Carolina. He was one of the most universally loved musicians in Nashville. He always had a smile on his face, especially when he was performing, and that attitude was present in his playing. That was certainly one of the factors that contributed to his success. He also had a near-photographic memory, and, in this interview, he offers valuable insight into establishing a career and dealing with the challenges of the changing music industry.

To break the ice, let's start with growing up in Illinois.

I was born in Alton, Illinois, in the same hospital that Miles Davis and Clark Terry were born in—Alton Memorial Hospital. Of course, everybody knows Miles Davis grew up in East St. Louis, but he was actually born in the same hospital I was.

I grew up in Jerseyville, Illinois. I got my first drum at age five when I insisted on having a drum because of the Spike Jones and his City Slickers television show on Saturday nights. I always watched that at my dad's house (my mom and dad were divorced when I was four). Those guys were like the precursor to Zappa and the Mother's of Invention. They played wacky, crazy stuff. They could all read fly you-know-what and play different instruments. They *all* hit something throughout the show, whether it was tuned cowbells or whatever. I just fell in love with that.

We had a distant relative that played drums. He helped my parents get me a Slingerland wood field drum for my fifth birthday. They painted it the colors of the grade school I would be starting at soon at six years old. So it was red and white—red rims on top and bottom and white in the middle. I was lucky that I had a great musical director starting in the third grade. He taught elementary through high school bands. He was a clarinetist named Claude Smith. His office was below the stage, which was in the gymnasium in my elementary school.

He would teach from the Haskell Harr book. He used to tell me about Gene Krupa and the big bands. He turned me on to Neil Hefti charts back then, probably in the late fifties and early sixties. He [Smith] started a stage band in elementary school playing those Hefti charts. It was essentially pop music of the time arranged for a little school band. I was playing drum set in that group. I had a Slingerland Blue Sparkle four-piece kit. By the time I got to high school, I had gotten into Louie Bellson. I had a double-bass kit that was a blue sparkle kit with two eighteen-inch bass drums and double toms. I played "Wipeout" for the high school when the band would play at halftime of basketball games.

That really opened up my eyes more to music and the recording process. I read an article on Hal Blaine. I was surprised that Dennis Wilson wasn't playing on all of the Beach Boys records. This article was saying that he [Blaine] was playing on all of my favorite records from the sixties: the Mamas and the Papas, Jan and Dean, and all the West Coast things. So Hal Blaine has been a gigantic influence on me through my whole life. He put the spark in me at the age of thirteen or fourteen reading this article about him. I thought that it would be really fun to be playing on people's records. I had no idea how to go about that. It was already on "the hard drive," so to speak.

I was living in the St. Louis area. I went to William Jewell College in Liberty, Missouri, near Kansas City. I didn't major in music. I was a political science major, and then got out of that. I got discouraged with that and left school. I went back to my hometown area.

I loved Kansas City. I didn't like the school. Moving back into the St. Louis area, I started playing locally with different bands. There was a guy named Phil Driscoll who was playing at the Chase Park Plaza Hotel. The drummer was a friend of mine named Ed Kotowski. I was playing percussion at this point. I was mainly getting into hand drums. I had gotten a set of Gon Bops congas and started listening and playing along with Mongo Santamaria records and other popular music of the time when I was maybe fouteen or fifteen years old.

Did you take lessons on congas?

No, I wound up meeting a man named Rich Tokatz. He's like my brother now. He was playing in a jazz club in St. Louis. We had a mutual friend named Phil Halsey. I'm sure a lot of drummers all over this country remember Phil Halsey. He was a Slingerland rep for a long time and ran Northland Music in St. Louis. There was a drum department downstairs. They had the best inventory of any drum or music store in the city. He became kind of like a surrogate father to me for many, many years.

I went into this club when I wasn't even old enough to get in. My mom would take me to see Phil playing drums and Rich Tokatz playing congas. Rich started teaching me congas. We got together a few times. He taught me how to get a slap and do the finger slide. All of it. That's how I got more into hand drumming.

In 1970 or 1971, I saw Phil Driscoll. He had a great bunch of players from . . . three members of his band—Dick Sims on organ and kicked bass pedals and Jamie Oldaker on drums and Sergio Pastora on percussion (congas, timbales, all that stuff). My friend Ed and I would go down to catch happy hour. We were working the same hours they were at a different club downtown. We'd get inspired to go play. Those guys left Driscoll's band to go with Bob Seger before playing with Eric Clapton.

Were those guys also from the St. Louis area?

No, they were from Tulsa. Driscoll was from Tulsa, but he brought these players in. They left, so Phil went back and got a new bunch of players that learned from those guys: a drummer by the name of Rick "Moon" Calhoun—he was the original drummer for Rufus years later; Carl Pickard on organ and kick pedals; Rick Bielke was a guitar player from Tulsa. Then he had auditions for an auxiliary guy to play bass, trumpet, keyboard, and stuff. Felix Robinson from St. Louis got that gig. I got the percussion gig.

We played with Phil [Phil Driscoll and Yurmama] from around the end of 1971 into 1973. I went to California to do a record with him. I immediately turned around because they weren't going to pay us for doing the record. I had already done some recording in St. Louis and knew that there was a union. They were not going to pay us. I didn't think that was right, so I went back.

A friend that I met through Phil, Charlie Chalmers, lived in Memphis. We went to Knox Phillips's place. He's the great Memphis record producer Sam Phillips's son. Knox had a studio, and we had cut some tracks with Phil Driscoll there. I met Charlie Chalmers through that.

Charlie insisted that I needed to leave Phil. So I went to Memphis and played on some stuff that he [Charlie] was producing. He then convinced me that I really needed to move to Muscle Shoals to play with Roger Hawkins.

Pardon me for interrupting. In regards to the Phil Driscoll situation, the record label wasn't going to pay you?

Well, Phil Driscoll and his backer were going to pay $350 a week to live on. We would be working all day and night on recording. So I knew that wasn't right. I made the decision that, even though I loved playing with Phil, it wasn't going to be a good thing.

That's why I wound up taking Charlie's suggestion and going down and working. I went back to St. Louis and then went down to Memphis. I worked with a couple of musicians from Muscle Shoals in Memphis, with Charlie producing this stuff. James Hooker, who played piano with Nancy Griffith (he still does, I think), was there, and so was the bass player Bob Wray. They told some people in Muscle Shoals about me. They started flying me down for some sessions from St. Louis.

What kind of percussion rig did you have back then?

Congas, timbales . . . I had a bunch of shakers and tambourines—that kind of stuff . . . cabasas, you know. I remember one of the first sessions I did at Rick Hall's Fame Studios. They put a song up, and I asked them from my booth to wait while I tuned up. There was a silence from the control room. The voice of Larry Henby, the engineer, came over the headphones. He asked, "You mean you can tune those things?" I said, "Yeah, you can tune them" [laughs]. They had never known that. Occasionally guys would play congas, bongos, percussion on stuff, but nobody really knew that it isn't a bad idea to tune the drums for each track so they are sympathetic with the key.

I ended up moving to Muscle Shoals in 1973 in Florence, Alabama, which is part of the quad cities down there.

Before we move on to your time in Muscle Shoals, were you doing sessions in St. Louis at that time too?

Yeah, at Technosonic Studio. It was the Lester family studio. We did custom projects up in the city.

What kinds of tunes were those?

They went from gospel things to local commercials—jingles. Technosonic did a lot of those kinds of things. In fact, years later they were still doing a lot of the stuff. The Mayer brothers, who played with Jimmy Buffet, are from St. Louis, as well as Roger Guth. They all worked at Technosonic.

Was that a valuable learning time?

Yes, it was. At the same time they started flying me to Muscle Shoals, I was working on sessions in St. Louis. Finally, I made the decision to move to Muscle Shoals. I loved St. Louis. I still do, but it's a rather challenging city for a musician to make a living in. It always has been, even though there have been great players. Michael McDonald is from St. Louis and lots of other guys.

Did you work with him back then?

Michael was [laughs] . . . My senior year in high school I was in charge of getting the music, the band, together for the senior prom. I hired a band called Jerry Jay and the Sheratons. They were a soul band with horns. Michael was the keyboard player. He can be seen playing a Farfisa in my senior high school yearbook.

Then I played in a different band that was managed by the same people, the Pokorny family, that managed Jerry Jay and the Sheratons after Michael had moved to Los Angeles. I was in a band playing for Joe Pokorny.

I've got a lot of fond memories of St. Louis. Michael and I have talked about it quite a bit. The last time I saw him—I started working with Aretha [Franklin] over the course of the last six or seven years. I guess we did the big music festival in Memphis that they have every spring or summer. Michael and I got to chat quite a bit because he was playing after us. One of the first things he said was, "Yeah, I've got to be the one to follow Aretha Franklin" [laughs]. He's a great guy. He's got a killer band.

Our paths kind of crisscrossed over the years. I worked for Paul Anka from '75 to '81 and '85 to '89. I played on "You're Having My Baby" [on *Anka*, released in 1974], which is how I got hooked up with him down in Muscle Shoals. Michael was, for a short period of time, writing with Paul Anka.

Chuck Sabatino was also in that picture in my high school yearbook with Michael McDonald. Chuck was one of my good friends when I moved to Los Angeles in 1970. He and I knew each other back in St. Louis. We became better friends in L.A. He was in Michael's band. He had a higher register, same kind of voice, than Michael and could sing the higher harmony parts. He played keyboards, bass, drums, guitar . . . everything. He was a wonderful guy who has unfortunately passed away. So our [McDonald's and Roady's] paths crossed.

So you moved to Muscle Shoals.

Yeah, I moved in 1973 to play in all of the studios, and I did play in all of them—Wish Bone, Broadway, Fame—but *the* place was Muscle Shoals Sound. That was owned by four musicians that started the studio. The history of that rhythm section and that studio goes from [Bob] Seger to the Rolling Stones to Rod Stewart to Paul Simon to the Staple Singers—you name it, it was cut in this old building that used to be a casket factory.

It was this little, one-room studio with burlap walls that could be moved around to isolate instruments. There was a vocal booth and a drum booth. That's where I *really* learned how to play in a recording studio. I played on pretty much a daily basis with Roger Hawkins, who I love. He taught me more about what I've been doing for the last forty years than anybody.

What types of things do you feel you learned from him?

He taught me how to listen, and how to play off of what you're hearing. He taught me when to lay out—what not to play is just as important as knowing what and where to play.

Was Roger vocal about that, or did you pick it up by being around him?

We would just talk about different things. Mainly what I learned was playing live with him and listening to him. My whole thing was that he and David Hood would be locked as bass and drums. I needed to fit my little pieces and kind of create and choreograph my parts to work with what he [Roger] was doing.

Were you still using the Gon Bops congas at that point?

I still have those same Gon Bops.

Were you using bongos and other instruments too?

In 1971, I think, I got a set of blonde Gon Bops congas with the tear-dropped hardware. At the same time, they made me a set of triple bongos. They were seven-inch, eight-inch, and nine-inch bongos. I had them mounted and used them for years. I still have the nine-inch drum, and the congas.

What other gear were you using?

I had timbales and had picked up a lot of different toys—mark trees, bell trees, lots of shakers, tambourines, and started making my own shakers. There was a place on the border of Sheffield, Alabama, and Tuscumbia (they kind of all run together—Muscle Shoals, Florence, Sheffield, and Tuscumbia), and it was two stories called Plow Boys. The best way to describe it was an indoor Sanford and Son [laughs]. There were old dishwashers, washing machines . . . just things everywhere. I would take mallets and sticks and hit on stuff. I remember finding a couple of those round aluminum sleds that kids played with back then. They were dented, and if you suspended them you could get different pitches out of the different dents. I bought all kinds of stuff like that.

I started collecting junk and making shakers out of film cans and pop cans. I put rocks in Fanta Grape Soda cans. I got into being inventive.

We would get some rather eclectic artists coming through. Laura Nero would describe her music in colors—that kind of thing. Artists have a different way of communicating what they're hearing.

We were doing an Art Garfunkel album. How that came to be was very interesting. The guys at Muscle Shoals Sound tried to get me on every artist's album. They'd mention that they had a great guy for percussion. So Paul Simon was coming in with Art Garfunkel for two days. They had been apart for many years. They got together for a song called "My Little Town." It was their one collaboration. They were both there, and I worked on that mainly just sitting around until they finally had to leave on the second day. They *let* me put what I wanted to put on it, which was bongos, I think cowbell . . . and I can't remember exactly. I had, like, ten minutes to come up with a part because they had to get to Huntsville to fly to New York for the Grammy Awards. So they wanted to get back.

So I put my parts down. I got paid for two days for all of the sessions. Then when the record came out I had been replaced by Ralph Mac-Donald—*Ralph MacDonald!* He was my idol. That was the guy that, as a percussionist . . . Hal Blaine was the inspiration, but as a percussionist, Ralph MacDonald has always been the epitome of taste, time, and feel. He is legendary for his perfect time. So I was being replaced by the one guy that I couldn't argue with. I found comfort that he played the same instruments that I chose. No one told me what to play. Ralph just did it his way. All my parts were there; they were just played by Ralph like he would. It was kind of a bummer, *but* Barry Beckett wound up producing an Art Garfunkel solo record called *Watermark* that I played on shortly after. It was all Jimmy Webb tunes.

So he came back to Muscle Shoals a few months later, and I was in on all of those sessions. To this day, that's one of the records that I'm most proud of. It's subtle percussion. There's one song—I've talked about this in other interviews—called "Marionette." They wanted the sound of marionettes kind of clacking together. I had some bamboo wind chimes. I tried that, and Art said that wasn't quite right because they sound hollow. Bamboo chimes *are* hollow. Marionettes are solid, carved wood.

Roger Hawkins had a box of thirty or forty old whittled down 5B drumsticks in a back closet. Most of them were plastic tip, but they were all whittled down at the shoulder. I just got some string and strung up about thirty of them on a couple of microphone boom stands, and that's what is on the record. Sure enough, it's solid. That's the creative part of what I got to do down there.

They let me do pretty much what I felt. Artists would suggest something sometimes, but I pretty much had free rein of what I would come up with.

You got to spend some personal time with Art Garfunkel during those sessions. What was that like?

It was great. He came in with Jimmy Webb for the first group of sessions. They would put me and Art up in the Holiday Inn. We would just drive over to the studio in one car—back and forth. It was really interesting. He's a very smart man. I really enjoyed hanging out and listening to this very intelligent man talk about a lot of different stuff, from politics to music.

One of the most memorable nights of my career was when *Hotel California* came out. You couldn't get a copy of that in Muscle Shoals. That was probably in 1977. We sent a runner over to Hunstville, Alabama, to [laughs] buy the record. He brought it back, and after everybody left, they let us stay in the studio and listen to the record using the turntable in the control room. He and I listened to that record top to bottom, both sides. That was back when they had *two sides* to a record [laughs].

It was very interesting because he knew Glenn Frey and some of those guys through the business. I remember that he would lift the needle after almost every cut and would talk about something musical about it—something that reminded him of something else. It was a really interesting after-hours thing getting to hang with him.

In my whole career, I've gotten a lot of gold and platinum records from artists. His, although I don't have it anymore, was the only gold record that I got a personally handwritten letter thanking me for. To me, that says a lot about who Art is. You hear different stories about their "tumultuous" relationship, he and Paul [Simon], but Art—it was a fun time. I'm very, very proud of that record.

You were really busy in Muscle Shoals for a long time.

Yeah, it was a fun time period. I moved there in 1973, as I mentioned, and I didn't leave until the end of '78. I moved back to St. Louis, but I continued to work in Muscle Shoals after 1978. I would fly in from

Los Angeles for certain things too. Disco was just starting to come in, and this was before drum machines. Percussion was on a lot of recordings. "Turn the Beat Around"—all kinds of disco had percussion—congas, shakers, tambourines. It was loaded up.

Those years were busy and great financially because they hadn't really come up with drum machines until the late seventies. When I moved to Los Angeles, the Bee Gees were on top, and I got really blessed to do an Andy Gibb album.

I was living in Los Angeles. Ron and Howard Albert were brothers that were producers. They were doing Pure Prairie League. The record I played on was the first record that Vince Gill was on with Pure Prairie League. I didn't meet him at the time. They flew me in to overdub the whole album. That was at Criteria Recording Studios in Miami, and they were working on an Andy Gibb record in one of the other studios.

Albhy Galuten came over to our studio and asked if I would put a shaker on an Olivia Newton-John/Andy Gibb duet. I said, "Yeah, by all means." I took a whole bunch of my shakers over and we did that. Barry [Gibb] was there with Karl Richardson and Albhy in the control room. It was great. Here I am playing a shaker, but it's an Andy Gibb record! I'm thinking, "Wow! This is hot!" You know, you're hearing the Bee Gees all the time, and Andy had a good career going. They told me that they would fly me back in a few weeks when they had a few tracks done. Sure enough, they flew me and all my gear to Miami from Los Angeles. I got to spend a couple of days working on the rest of the record. So, yeah, I moved to Los Angeles at the end of 1978, and this would have been in 1979. That record was called *After Dark*. I'm very proud to be on it. It has excellent production, and it was an amazing musical team— Albhy, Karl, and Barry.

Do any songs from that record stick out to you?

There was a song called "Desire." "After Dark" was another radio song. I had just moved from St. Louis to Los Angeles. They actually approached me about moving to Miami. I wasn't about to move down there so soon. I thought about it briefly, but I had moved to Los Angeles in order to play on Quincy Jones records and different stuff out there. That was the whole point of moving out there. I wanted to be on different kinds of records. Muscle Shoals was definitely R&B. That's what we did, and they still do. It may have a country tinge or a rock tinge, but it's definitely rhythm and blues.

When you got to Los Angeles . . .

I had a gig with Paul Anka. I worked for him from 1975 to 1981. I moved at the end of 1978 during that stint with him.

Was it very easy to meet players out there through Paul's gig?

I wound up *almost* working out there those four years more when I wasn't there. I would be flown in when I was in Las Vegas. Jerry Wexler flew me in for an Etta James record that I overdubbed. I went in to do all kinds of stuff. The producers from Muscle Shoals would go to Los Angeles and put me on stuff because I was on the road. They would get me while I was on the West Coast or in Vegas and get me for the day and fly me back for my night gig. There were a couple of times when they just got me plane tickets for early in the morning, and I'd be back on a six p.m. plane to Vegas to play the eight p.m. show with Anka. I would then do the same thing the next day. That only happened a few times.

They would get some rental gear for me. They were great. R&R Express was my cartage company. That was the company that James Taylor and all of his players used—Leland Sklar, Jeff Porcaro, Jim Gordon.

Did you see those guys around?

Oh, yeah! I would run into them. It was funny. Leland and I didn't really hang out a lot until years later when I was living here [Nashville] and we were playing on sessions together. We met at an airport in Dallas. I went up and talked to him and told him that I had my gear at Bob and Ray's place, R&R Express, and my name is Tom Roady. He says, "*TROADY! TROADY!*" while pointing at me. And I said, "Leland, it has a big *T* followed by a dot." I had these silver cases with this big blue *T* followed by a dot and *ROADY*. They did the stenciling. But he said, "You're *TROADY*" [laughs]!

The last nine, ten months that I lived in Los Angeles were some of the . . . it was kind of mixed. I got the opportunity to play with Don Randy and Quest at the Baked Potato. I would go in and sit in. I did that one time. The bass player was a friend of mine and told Don to let me come in. Don invited me back and told me to plan on being there on Wednesdays through Saturdays. That was the premier gig for any player because of the visibility. It was, arguably, the number one jazz club, but it was a lot more than that. On Fridays and Saturdays, you couldn't get in the place. Lines waiting outside—it was the place.

One of my regrets, when I moved to Nashville, was leaving that gig behind. At that time, I was making two hundred dollars a week playing jazz Wednesday to Saturday night, but that didn't pay a $1,300-per-month mortgage.

Were you doing sessions while you were at the Baked Potato?

No. I left Anka. . . . Well, let's say we left each other in 1981. For the next year or so, I worked with the Fifth Dimension. That was mainly in Vegas. I was living in Los Angeles, and I would drive to Vegas with my gear and play several weeks through the year with them. I didn't do a whole lot of touring. They didn't carry a percussionist on tour. Mainly they got long twenty-week contracts in Vegas. They were great people. It was fun music to play, and great people. That's really what that was about.

Leaving to move to Nashville, leaving the Baked Potato gig, that was very—I missed it. The first six months here, I was wondering what I was doing.

Did you get a chance to interact with Jeff Porcaro?

I got to see Jeff. We met quite a few times. We knew each other, but I played on maybe three or four things that he was on. I was always overdubbing. I got to see him play live lots and lots of times at the Baked Potato. I remember for about six weeks straight, every Sunday night, Greg Mathieson, a great keyboard player, he, [Steve] Lukather, and Pops Popwell on bass (who now lives here in Nashville), they would take over the Baked Potato and play *rock 'n' roll*. It was very contemporary, L.A. instrumental rock. You couldn't get in the place. Sometimes Lenny Castro would sit in with them, and it was always great.

It was great playing with Don Randy and Quest. Don still owns the Baked Potato (or his son does, I guess). When you work for Don, you could always come in through the kitchen. You could stand by the bar if it was sold out. It didn't make any difference. You were kind of like family because you were playing there Wednesday through Saturday. The bartenders, the waitresses, and cooks could always come in and find standing room. I heard a lot of great players there.

Jeff Porcaro was a really open guy. I remember laughing with him. He had a great smile and a terrific laugh. On those nights when they were playing, sweat would be dripping off of them, and he would be just so in the pocket. He was always nice to me, and he didn't know me except that I was playing with Don. He was genuinely a wonderful guy.

What I have found throughout my career is that when I've met drummer heroes of mine, 99 percent of them are really nice guys. They are genuinely open to talking about anything, making you feel like family. Larrie Londin, God rest his soul, he would always make anybody that he met feel like they knew him. Your attitude and openness toward other players, you know, it's what we need to do. We need to pass it on—whatever information, even if it's just stories about players and experiences. Ultimately, that's what you've got. Sure, I've played on a lot of records and I'm very proud of that, but the stories, and the musicians that I've had the opportunity to play with, hang, and call friends, is really what we take away with us.

What led to your decision to move to Nashville?

When I lived in Muscle Shoals, I worked in Nashville. I would drive up for different things. One of my favorite recordings that I sent you not too long ago was the Wilson Pickett *Chocolate Mountain* record. We just got a copy recently. Ernie Winfrey, the engineer, sent us all (the ones that are still around) copies of that record. It's so funky. As many people have pointed out,about the photo that I put on Facebook, there is only one black guy, Wilson Pickett, and all the rest are white guys [laughs]. It's about the funkiest record you'll ever hear in your life.

It had Larrie Londin, Reggie Young, Mike Leech, Bobby Woods, Pete Carr, and me. Pete and I were from Muscle Shoals. Bobby Woods, Mike Leech, and Reggie are Memphis guys. Larrie came from Detroit. So you've got three major R&B areas represented and everything that those players picked up in their careers to that point. That's why that record sounds the way it does.

I came back to be closer to Muscle Shoals. That's the whole reason I moved to Nashville. I didn't want to go to New York. It was a jungle, and I knew that. I felt like in L.A., other than the Baked Potato and a few good memories of stuff, I wasn't going to break into the Quincy Jones–type sessions.

I moved back to Nashville in 1982. I was never a big country music fan. Sorry about that, but I'm not. I thought that I'd get some work in Muscle Shoals. At one point, just to make a living, I was in seven different local bands at the same time. It was a booking nightmare just trying to deal with it all.

They weren't all country bands.

No. One of the best bands I was ever in was called the Nerve. I was in it from 1982 through around 1986. I went back on the road with Paul Anka in 1985. I was gone so often I had to leave the band. That band had Michael Rhodes playing bass, Danny Rhodes on guitar, Mike Lawler on keyboards, Ricky Rector played guitar too, and Jamie Nichol was playing congas.

What was so funny was that I moved to Nashville on Labor Day in 1982. The first week I was in town, I went to a movie theater out in Lions Head Village. I heard this reggae music through the walls while the movie was going on. So I walked around the corner after the movie was over, and I see this Catfish [banner]. It was this singer and group. Jamie Nichol was playing. I knew it had to be him the second I saw there was a conga player. He had played with Charlie Daniels on "The Jam," and some Dan Fogelberg records. I knew who he was. This was like the first week I was in town.

He invited me to come out the next weekend to hear this band he was in, the Nerve. So I went to this club called the Sutler, and they were playing. I was blown away. My friend Mark Morris, who was a percussionist in town at the time, was sitting in with them. I said, "Man, move over. Let me play!" The next time, Jamie told me to bring my stuff. I played one time, and the next thing I knew, Danny Rhodes invited me to a rehearsal.

This was very odd because they already had a percussionist. They were a six-piece band, and they were adding another guy—another mouth to feed. When you're getting three dollars a person at the door, adding a player takes away from the "general fund," so to speak. I played in that band for four years. It was all original stuff. . . . Well, mostly original stuff. They were playing Little Feat/Neville Brothers–type stuff.

Michael and Danny Rhodes were from Monroe, Louisiana, so they had that Louisiana thing.

Are they brothers?

No, no relation. They are just lifelong friends and from the same hometown.

So I moved here after playing with Don Randy and listening to music in clubs in L.A. The Nerve was the only band in the first few weeks that I was here that I paid the cover to see more than one time. It wasn't that I felt like I was a musical snob or anything, it was just after seeing Jack Mack and the Heart Attack with Jeff Porcaro and everything—it wasn't the same until I saw the Nerve. The next thing I knew I weaseled myself into a band that already had a percussionist [laughs].

So now we had two percussionists, drums, two guitars, keyboards, and bass.

Who was the drummer?

Kirby Shelstad. He's still a dear friend. We've been friends for thirty years. He's got a studio in West Meade. We talk every week. We hang out. He's an incredible tabla player. Very great drummer.

The best thing about that band was that Kirby would always take chances. He would try stuff, and I like that. It kept things fresh.

And that was your first real gig in town.

Yeah, them and a few other bands. I started doing some sessions. The first session I did was for Jimmy Bowen around 1983. That was a Conway Twitty *Merry Twistmas* when he had the Twitty bird. I played on several tracks on that.

Then I got asked to go back on the road in 1985 with Paul Anka. I had decided in January of that year that I was going to go back to school. I enrolled at Tennessee State University. I took piano, theory, and percussion with Tommy Davis. I got good grades. I completed the whole first year. I was all set to go back and continue with a full load. Then Anka called, and it was like four hundred dollars a week, which was more than I was making four years before when I left his band. All my teachers at TSU told me to go, letting me know that they'd be there when I got back. That's what the students are in school to do. I didn't go back, unfortunately.

As soon as I left, I started getting some calls for different projects that I was able to do until I left Anka's group again. I did some work in Muscle Shoals too. They were still doing some work there. In 1989, I got the opportunity to play on a couple Mark O'Connor records. The one we did, James Taylor was on a tracking session with Eddie Bayers, Jerry Douglas, John Jarvis, and Edgar Myer on bass. We did a couple songs for that record. James [Taylor] liked the configuration and had some small-venue stuff that he wanted to do with this band. He liked the violin, Dobro, and acoustic guitar combination. It was pretty much an "unplugged" thing that we were doing.

He told us that he'd be calling us. This was around the spring of 1989, and sure enough he did. Eddie couldn't do the tour because of other obligations. They decided to do the tour with just me. I knew that I wasn't going to pass up a James Taylor tour; it was six weeks, and there was nothing after that with him. I also knew that I had to tread delicately on my gig with Paul Anka. So I waited until what I thought was the right time. A month ahead of time, I requested to sub the show out. I had arranged a sub from Los Angeles, Danny Reyes (Walfredo Reyes Jr.'s brother).

Anka had three or four shows that conflicted with James Taylor's rehearsal schedule in New York City. They said, "No subs. Get out." The next day the conductor said that the official word was that I could do the recording with James Taylor. I said that it wasn't a recording, it was a tour. He replied that the point was that the moment I worked with James Taylor, I was out. I looked at him with the biggest grin of my whole entire life, and I said, "Perfect. You want it this way? Perfect." So that was the end of that run with Paul Anka.

It was one of those times where a musician knows that maybe once or twice in their career they are moving to something that's really going to be cool. The musician knows, but the other people don't know. That's what I wound up doing. I just shed like crazy on "Traffic Jam." I had my headphones on listening to Carlos Vega on live tapes. Once I did that tour, work really started picking up around 1989 to 1990. I started getting more calls for records here in Nashville.

Let's talk about your gear throughout the 1980s.

I didn't have any endorsements when I got the James Taylor thing. Larrie Londin helped me get the Sabian cymbal endorsement. That was my first one. I had already played on 350 records by that point, at least, from 1973 to 1980 something—probably more [records] than that. I never had a real endorsement deal. I was glad to get the Sabian deal. I kept telling them things that I was doing. I was sending them letters and leaving them messages for what turned out to be the wrong guy. My contact ended up being a Canadian marching percussion specialist at the company. I was going absolutely nowhere with them.

The straw that broke the camel's back was a Sabian advertisement in *Modern Drummer* around 1993 or 1994. It listed all of the Nashville drummers that were playing Sabian, and my name was nowhere to be found. I had been letting them know about my work playing on Suzy Bogguss and Vince Gill records. The ad came out and I was so upset.

The next day, literally, Rich Mangicaro from Paiste called me. I met him at a winter NAMM Show. I had given him a brief one-page résumé. He called and said that they were doing a photo shoot in Lieper's Fork and wanted to know if I wanted to be a Paiste artist. I said, "Yes!" So I let Sabian know, and Rich invited me to be part of the Paiste family. I still am an artist with them and am very proud of that.

What are some of your favorite sessions from the 1980s?

I remember more from the 1990s, actually. There was some work in the eighties for Warner Brothers, Gary Morris, and a few other things. I was just trying to build my way up. Around 1990 or 1991, things started picking up a lot more for me. I started doing work with Vince Gill, Trisha Yearwood . . . the Suzy Bogguss "Outbound Plane" record where the congas are so out front in the mix was a bit of a game changer for me personally. It was being heard, and I was being heard on radio. I still love Suzy's records. They're great. Carlos Vega is playing on a lot of that stuff. Eddie [Bayers] is on a lot of that stuff too.

In 1985, Paul Anka had gone out in Atlantic City. Tony Brown called me to do a Nicolette Larson session, and I couldn't do it. I said to him, "Man, I've wanted to work for you since I moved to town. Is this going to screw me?" He said no, but he finally called four or five years later. I reminded him of that, and he said, "See?" Yeah, but it was four or five years, man [laughs]!

Working with Garth Fundis on Trisha Yearwood stuff was a lot of fun. He would like to experiment. We would spend an hour finding the right place in Sound Emporium to record a cowbell on one of her records. We went from the loading dock to the hallway to the bathrooms. He would take the time to do that.

I worked with him on the New Grass Revival and some of those eighties records that he was producing. Those are some of the ones that I'm really proud of because it was just an incredible band. I got to do what I do on those records. That was a lot of fun.

Who were the drummers on those?

I'm sure Kenny Malone was on some of those.

What do you like about Kenny Malone's drumming?

Well, Kenny is just—he's just special. That's it. His playing is like nobody else. His human-being-ness, so to speak [laughs] . . . his personality. He's just a great guy and, once again, he gives it back. He will show you what he's doing. He'll talk about it. He'll tell you stories—talk about stories, man, he's got a million of them from the military days to everything.

Kenny's just a great guy. He's inventive. He always comes up with unique parts. He is the least boring drummer you will ever hear in your life. I mean that with all the love and respect. I love him. He doesn't play like anyone else. Not just in Nashville but anywhere.

How about Eddie Bayers Jr.?

Eddie! I love playing with Eddie. I played on lots of records in the eighties and nineties with him. I think, out of all of the drummers in town—especially after Larrie Londin passed . . . well, before we talk about Eddie. The thing about Larrie: if you went into a session and saw that Larrie was playing drums, you knew the drums were going to be killer, and that it was going to be wonderful. You also knew that you were going to have fun. You were going to laugh and have a great time because Larrie was there.

With Eddie: our pockets are in the same time/space frame. His backbeat will lay exactly where I feel. That goes back to Muscle Shoals playing with Roger Hawkins. They [Eddie and Roger Hawkins] have similar, but different, pockets. The time and feel thing, yeah, is there. I played on a lot of records with Eddie.

He and I went to Telluride [Bluegrass Festival] with James Taylor in 1990 and 1991. We did live shows together out there. Fortunately, I got to do drums and percussion when Eddie couldn't do that tour in 1989. I wish I would have had more elements. I didn't have a kick drum because they wanted it quiet. We played small theaters that were acoustically boomy. The sound level was quieter without a kick drum because the first thing, as you know, a sound man asks for is a kick drum. If there's no kick drum, then you go from there. Singers love it because the volume is low, they can hear themselves more naturally. But then again, glue-wise, I wish I would have had more control over that. That taught me a lot.

I think that Eddie is *musical*. His pocket is great, but what he plays is music. That comes from being a piano player before he was a drummer. I really believe that with all of my heart. Plus, he's always fun. You know it's going to be a good time when you walk into a session and he's there, just like it was with Larrie.

There are other guys—Paul Leim is one. He's got a different pocket, different feel. He can do it all, no doubt about it. He is a little more in front. I'm not going to say he's dry, but it's a different kind of space. I love a lot of guys. Greg Morrow is a wonderful drummer here in town. He sounds great on the Dixie Chicks stuff that I played on.

There are some really great drummers in this town.

What are the great drummer hangouts in town?

D.O.G. Percussion was owned by Larrie and Debbie Londin. That was their drum shop and was the place in the seventies and eighties to go and hang out. If you needded anything drum related, it was there, or Gary Forkum's place over in Berry Hill at the time. I went there a lot also.

You told me one time what "D.O.G." stood for.

His wife's name: Debbie O. Gallant. Gallant was Larrie's real last name. D.O.G. Percussion.

Was it a big store?

It was on 19th Avenue. It was a small shop. I remember that cool logo with a dog. He had a lot of inventory for being such a small place. It was always nice because somebody would always be coming in while you were there, like Tommy Wells picking up heads or sticks. It was a great place to hang. You felt welcome there. So it was small but nice.

Of course, Fork's was in town . . .

I forget what year Fork's moved from Berry Hill to 12th Avenue. It's expanded as he's grown through the years. His inventory is great. Now it's just one of the best drum shops in the country. That's a good thing because this town has a lot of drummers, and there are more moving here every day.

I get calls from people all the time wanting to know how to meet people and how to get into doing demos and stuff. I always try to give them my thoughts on it.

Who were the drummers in Paul Anka's band?

The first drummer was Chet Forrest [George "Chet" Forrest] from Las Vegas. Bud Harner played drums for a little while. Then, for about a year, we had two drummers that alternated from Los Angeles: Steve Shaffer from 1975 to 1981. He was on all kinds of television shows and studio work. The other drummer was Ralph Humphrey, who is on *Dancing with the Stars*. So it would be either Steve or Ralph, depending on who could make it.

It was a lot of fun. I remember a solo in Anka's show *Jubilation*. The drums rose up on a riser. I was on a riser behind him. The drums would go up past me, and I'd just sit there. Ralph would play a solo every night, and he never repeated himself. It was always just unbelievable. Anka always wanted you to watch him [Anka] at the end so he could cut the song. Ralph refused to look at him. He just kept playing. So Anka would bring the band in and cut them off. And Ralph would just keep going [mimics a big, rumbling ending] [laughs]. Now he and Joe Porcaro have their school.

Jim Gordon, let's put it this way, he came in to do the Paul Anka gig, but it didn't happen. Bud Harner couldn't do something, I believe, and they brought Jim Gordon into Vegas for a rehearsal. He had done some recording with Paul in Los Angeles. After the first hour, the first break, he went up to the conductor and (according to what I heard) told him that he needed to leave. The conductor said, "Well, you can't leave." Jim said, "I have to leave. I've been told that I need to leave." The conductor asked who told him. Jim wouldn't elaborate. You could see that something wasn't right. It wasn't really reflected in his playing. It was more of an air of not being all there. Not necessarily when he sat down to a drum set. I've only seen that kind of thing once or twice where you just know that something isn't right. I don't think it was even a year later when he kinda lost it and took his mother's life. It ended a remarkable career.

Had you met him before then?

Yeah, we had met at R&R Express. I knew who he was. I was a gigantic Jim Keltner fan. I still am. The *Mad Dogs and Englishmen* tour where they [Gordon and Keltner] were on that thing, and then, of course, the "Layla" piano part, which he [Gordon] played and wrote. . . . He was an incredibly talented guy. It's one of the unfortunate stories. It seems like there are a lot of unfortunate stories that go along with drummers. His is one of the more tragic ones. Jeff's [Porcaro] death.

Carlos Vega, who I loved and I did quite a few records with like Vince Gill and Suzy Bogguss. Jimmy Bowen would bring him in for different stuff.

Carlos and I became good friends. Right after I had done the James Taylor tour—I had seen Carlos play in Karizma. I saw them at the Baked Potato all the time. Carlos and I didn't get to know each other until he started coming in to Nashville for sessions. Every time he came in, we'd hang. He came out to my house. I loved the guy, man. We loved to hang out. I wish I could have done the James Taylor gig playing percussion with him on drums. That would have been a huge thing for me. I love James with Russ Kunkel, but seeing and hearing Carlos (especially when Carlos and Leland Sklar were doing it) was something else. When Carlos and Leland were playing with James, it was just awesome and tight.

Did you talk to Carlos in that last year before he passed?

Yeah. We probably worked together once or twice in that year before he passed away. He would come in for different sessions. Even if I wasn't on the sessions with him, he would call and we would go hang out. I'd come over to the studio and say hello.

Carlos was wonderful. He played with Olivia Newton-John with some friends of mine that were in that band. We knew each other quite a bit when I lived in Los Angeles but never got a chance to work together until Nashville.

The nineties really picked up for you in terms of session work.

Yeah. Like it or not, Garth [Brooks] brought a lot of different kind of notoriety to country music back then. There were so many people making good records at that time. I'm very fortunate to have been on a lot of those. It started slowing down for me around 2000 or 2001. That's just the nature of the business.

What are some of your favorite rooms or places to work around town? Do you have a favorite room?

Yeah, without a doubt. My favorite room was Emerald Studio, which is on 16th Avenue. I think I did a lot of Suzy Bogguss records there. I worked at the Sound Shop too, but Emerald was the place that a bunch of us did all of the CNN Headline News bumpers for eight years or so. They would come up three or four times a year and spend a couple of days recording all those bumpers and cues. Most of those were done at

Emerald. I liked that room because you could see everybody. The glass walls let you see two rooms over into the piano booth. It was a great room to cut tracks because of the visual communication.

The Rock Room at Masterphonics, which they called "the tracking room." That's where we did the photo shoot for my *Modern Drummer* article. It had a wall that was made out of rock—it still does. I did a lot of work at Sound Shop and enjoyed that—Brooks & Dunn and a whole bunch of different records were made there. Sound Stage is another great room. Jimmy Bowen used that place a lot at one of the two studios in there.

What were some of the more wild sounds you were getting on those records?

The wild sounds started in Muscle Shoals getting different pieces of junk and stuff. Talk about wild sounds, we were doing a Mac McAnally album in the seventies. A sax player friend of mine from Anka's band brought me two fire bells from an old fire station in Bakersfield that was torn down. They were these big, old red fire bells. I got a dish pan and a coat hanger and I suspended them. I played all that stuff with mallets while I dipped them in water. On the same song, I had a waterphone, which is played with a bow. It has rods attached to a covered metal bowl that has water in it. The mastering company called the producer and asked if he wanted the feedback noise removed from this song. It sounded like screeching whales, and it was at the top of the song. He [the producer] laughed and said he wanted it kept in there. Those were some strange sounds.

Being on the road traveling with Anka allowed me to go to drum shops all over the place. I would pick up different things. One of my favorite shops was owned by Ray Ayotte in Vancouver called Drums Only. That was probably the best drum shop I was ever in. He had inventory everywhere. There were all kinds of exotic instruments from the Middle East and Africa.

Getting into electronics changed a lot for me. I bought my first drum machine, which kind of sucked me into the electronic percussion world. I owned DrumKats and MalletKats, but I never bought a Roland kit. I had a DynaSonic kit and a Yamaha electronic kit, which was actually pretty cool. We were doing FM synthesis for percussion. That was very interesting. Pads were terrible, though. They would hurt because they were so hard. Those Simmons pads would send a shock up and down your arm.

In 1994, the Zendrum came out. That let me bring other sounds into different stuff. I played Zendrum on a Wynonna Judd record.

How do the samples from the nineties hold up to you over time?

The main box we used with the Zendrum was the Alesis D4. Then they came out with the DM5 and then the DM Pro. The record I did in 1996 called *Zendrum One Tribe* had all the drum sounds from an E-mu Emax or the Alesis boxes. I got hooked up pretty good with E-mu during the mid- to late nineties, and they gave me a bunch of different modules and things.

I remember doing one record at Trevecca University in their chapel. Larrie Londin was playing drums. I brought my MalletKat, DrumKat, and my rack of gear. Larrie had his rack of gear. We were playing a lot of electronic samples.

I still love electronics. That's part of what I do.

You work with Korg these days, right?

Well, I'm a Korg artist, but very low level. I've been with them since the 1970s, really. I met Joan [Aupperlee] when I was out with Anka. She helps me out when I want to get something from them. I've been very blessed with endorsement things. The Zendrum relationship is wonderful, of course, and the E-mu relationship was great. I don't think they're [E-mu] in business anymore.

I am honored to be with Paiste all of these years. I was with Mapex from 1997 to around 2000 or 2001. I then became a DW drum set endorser. I just left Toca recently after probably seventeen or eighteen years. I love Toca instruments, but I'm a Natal endorser now. Natal is a UK company that's been around since 1965. My friend Danny Jarrett is the U.S. marketing and Artist Rep. He asked me if I would be an artist, and I love the Cubano series and congas that I've got. I've got a set of the Fusion series congas to play live. We're waiting on a drum kit from them.

You've been playing pop percussion for a very long time. You mentioned learning from Richard Tokatz. How much time have you spent exploring the traditional rhythms of different percussion instruments?

I haven't done as much exploration of technique as I would have liked. I feel that it requires a lot of time. Up until the last few years, I've been a pretty busy guy making a living. I respect players that have gone to Cuba and learned all the stuff. No one in a recording session that I've been on has asked me to play a guaguancó or even a rhumba. It hasn't necessarily come up. Now, I *can* play a guaguancó and rhumba, but I'm not as dedicated to learning the history and such. I take what knowledge I've got from other players, like Rich Tokatz, Larrie Londin, Roger Hawkins . . . from anybody and try to work what knowledge I picked up from them into what I do and how I play.

Obviously, some rhythms and beats aren't going to work in country songs. Generally speaking, I tend to play simple and make my part, whatever it is, fit with everything from the rhythm guitar to bass and the drummer. It isn't just about locking in with drums. Hopefully we all know that. There's so much stress put on a percussionist locking in with the drummer. Yeah, that's part of it. The drums and everyone else are trying to lock in with each other. The greatest thing that I have developed through the years in playing with Roger Hawkins on a daily basis was the development of my ears. I've learned to hear parts, playing song forms enough times that I know that the bridge is coming up in four bars and that it's different from the rest of the song.

You need to modify your part. . . . Say it's a shaker part in 4/4 where you're accenting on two and four [sings part] on a verse. When it gets to the chorus or bridge section, you might want to move into straight accents on all four counts [sings part]. It will help drive and lift (that's a word we use a lot) a song into the next section, before you come to the turnaround, which is just a restatement of the intro of the song. Then you go back into the second verse and the original pattern. That really has very little to do with knowledge of traditional rhythms. You just have to know and hear where you're going, what will work, what *won't* work (that's a big, important thing), and to remember that your part is just one little bit of the *whole* recording of the song. You've got all the other parts going on, and you want to complement them. Sometimes you want to play off them, but not necessarily duplicate them.

I hate when I'm playing with a drummer, and I play something, and he'll play a fill right after. It's not about call and answer. It's about the song, the singer, and the songwriter. It's that kind of thing. You're going to bring your ego to a session or song, to a degree, but you don't want to let your ego overshadow what you're bringing to it and what everybody else is bringing to it.

What musical attributes do you feel are important for a successful musician?

Number one: a desire and passion to play. If you don't have that *passion* to give you the drive and the desire to continue to play music because you *have to* (as part of your soul), then don't. From a drummer or percussionist standpoint, it all comes down to (and [Steve] Gadd's talked about this) time, feel, and taste. It's a mixture of those three things that should always be at the forefront. It's not about fills, crash cymbals, or drum parts. You need to be able to sit back and enjoy other people's contributions to whatever song you're trying to record. We're fortunate that we have good sound systems with cue systems that allow you to hear everything and even get your own individual mix in most cases. You can hear all of the other parts. It's not about drum solos.

I think what I did through a lot of my career, especially early on in Muscle Shoals, was play off lyric. Certain things, like on the Art Garfunkel album, or words would give a visual like a finger cymbal or little triangle hit in the right spots. So when you're listening, you're not just listening to the bass player, guitar player, or keyboards. You have to listen to the lyric. I'm not one to listen to lyrics on the radio, but I do when I'm recording a song. I'm very aware in that environment.

You have to have a certain amount of chops, but they aren't the thing that's going to get you in the door. It's your creativity and how you work that creativity in with time, feel, pocket, and . . . your *attitude*. The attitude that you have in playing your instrument, in working with people—you want people to enjoy working with you and being around you. You don't want to be a complainer. Yeah, you still may work, but there are guys in town that, you love them and they play great, but, at some point, they're going to be a pain in the butt. I'm sorry! What am I doing [laughs]? I need to be careful that I don't call somebody out! The thing is that they're good at what they do, and they work in spite of themselves, in some cases.

Your attitude and showing people a smile, laughing, having a good time. Sharing a joke and laughing. It's music. It's not high finance. Lord knows it's not that [laughs]. It's music and it's meant to be fun. It's meant to free the spirit of the person listening, and certainly the player's spirit. You should, whether it's a sad or happy song, be emotional. You should try to be as creative as you can within the boundaries that you're placed in.

How has the industry changed over the last thirty years?

David Hungate's quote on Facebook says it all for me. David ran into an old friend, and the friend said, "David, I haven't seen you in a long time. Are you still in the music business?" And David answered, "Yeah, I'm just waiting to see how it ends" [laughs]. It's very double-edged, but it's true.

The business has changed a lot. The perceived value and quality of music has declined in the last ten years. Sadly, it's declined to a point where I listen to NPR most of the time or XM—maybe the Spa channel or Smooth Jazz station. The double-edged sword of that is that the business end has taken such a hit that when a record comes out like Adele's *21*, it just shines so brightly. You just can't ignore it. My wife turned me on to her [Adele] last year. Unfortunately, we can't get tickets to the sold out Ryman show. Those kinds of musical things just stand out more now because of all the crap that they're surrounded by. It just makes them even better, if you will, or at least more noticeable that they are outstanding.

I was talking to somebody the other day. I just got the newest Doobie Brothers record. It's a killer record. Fifteen years ago, three or four songs on there would have been heard on the radio *all the time*. That record would be a multiplatinum seller. Now you can hardly even hear it unless you happen to hear it on XM or something. If you like the Doobie Brothers, this is as good as any of their past records.

It's sad that they're out there, but unless you have a particular artist that you follow and look for on iTunes when their new records come out, it's word of mouth. I'm a huge Deep Forest fan. I used to hear them on United Airlines commercials. Now, even though it's basically one person, I still look forward to another record each time. Those things stand out still.

Look at Lady Gaga. Whether she's just a revamp of Madonna—they're both very talented women. Yeah, she's wild and crazy with the hats and outfits, but unfortunately the audience that she is aspiring to have likes that. Where the rest of us, it's more about the music. I would dig her even more if she was just playing the piano and not doing the "Lady Gaga" thing. She's really talented. I can see her talent; for anybody that really digs deep enough, it's there.

She reminds a little of Elton [John]. His talent shone through in spite of the glasses and the whole thing. There are some very similar career things going on. I guess she's [Lady Gaga] the godmother of Elton and his partner's child. I think that good music definitely shines through; it's just that there's so little that we're actually getting to hear these days.

What do you tell players or people who want to get into the industry?

The Wrecking Crew movie pointed out to me that, as my career has gone the last ten years or so, their careers went that way too. That movie is an unbelievable documentary—all of my musical heroes from my youth are represented in this, at the Belcourt Theater. It really drove home how the industry changed. I forget who said it in the movie, but it said that they [the Wrecking Crew] had their time. For them, it was the mid- to late 1960s to around 1980 or 1985. That was their time when the hits and studio players were in demand. The amount of recordings that they did is just unbelievable.

Those guys, along with some of the New York players like Richard Tee, Bernard Purdie, Ralph MacDonald, and [Steve] Gadd—the East Coast guys—experienced the change of the recording business. The recording business changed so much that you're not going to have that kind of gathering of talent in one room. I mean, the photos that they had of the Wrecking Crew had twenty or twenty-five people in the studio. There are six guitar players on those sessions. There weren't any overdubs or anything. Everybody had their parts. Wow. Talk about pressure!

You have your run, however long it is—ten, fifteen, or twenty years with a lot of work—and then it goes away. As much as I tell myself that it's an age thing, it isn't. It's just how the business of recording music changes.

I remember the 'N Sync days. You could look on the back of an 'N Sync record and couldn't even tell who was actually playing what instrument. It was people from Norway, and there was programming and assistant programming. That was the height of that process. There's a little less of that now, except maybe in rap, which I don't really follow.

I think a young player can't really expect to make a living as I chose to my whole career playing on people's records. There isn't enough of that anymore. You have to be able to do it all. You have to be able to self-promote, go out on the road, play around town, and produce. Anybody that aspires to do studio work has to have their own home studio. You have to sink the money into it. There are so many drummers, seeing as how we're talking about drummers, in this town that have them [home studios], and have had them for a long time. Steve Brewster was one of the first guys to have a place that he could record himself. That's when I decided that I needed to get one too. So I moved from a place I had been living for fourteen years to a place on the other side of town that had a basement that's twenty-five by twenty-five feet with a high ceiling. I'm able have a studio that I built to put myself on other people's projects. That doesn't mean that I'm doing a lot of Music Row stuff. Some of my friends have studios that are doing some of that, but I'm recording projects for people all over the world.

My advice to young players is to network—get out and meet as many people as you can. They definitely have to be able to play the instrument really well, without a doubt. And they need to look at pursuing recording, but learn more about the art of recording—engineering. Somebody told me yesterday that everything is going to Logic instead of ProTools. I'm thinking, "Hey, I've got seven years invested in ProTools!"

This is something interesting. ProTools offers a great program for songwriters, musicians, and engineers. They have several different levels of accreditation—ProTools Certification. They don't offer that songwriting course in Nashville, which has, per capita, the most songwriters in the country. And I think, "Why?" The courses aren't cheap, whether they are two, five, or ten days. It's a big chunk of change.

I'm seriously considering going to Atlanta to do a five-day thing there because I want to learn more about the program, especially since I moved to ProTools 9 from version 7. I had been going along now pretty well, but I need to get deeper without having to call all my friends and ask questions about how my I/O [Input/Output] setup has changed, for example. That's one of the things that young players need to do, and that's expand their knowledge of the technology that creates the music these days.

I've said it many, many times, that I wished I had paid more attention to the unbelievable engineers that I worked with throughout the years. Then again, their process and what they did on analog tape back then—I mean, the basics are still there in digital, but the tools and everything else have changed so much. Many of the guys that I worked with have moved to digital, though.

I think learning the process, acquiring a way to record yourself, and having good networking skills are key. Networking is a fine line. You don't want to be a pain in the butt to somebody. There's one guy who I won't name that's on Facebook and isn't from Nashville. Almost all of his posts are blatant self-promotion, and it's almost to the point where you want to get rid of it. It's the same stuff over and over several times a day. So network carefully in a manner that isn't annoying and still gets the point across.

I feel very blessed to have played on a lot of records. I guess I'm bad about this, but when I see somebody that is a Facebook friend, we don't really know each other, and they post something like Sanford Thompson Band's "Smoke from a Distant Fire"—I can't stop myself from writing that I played percussion on it, and it's one of my favorite records. It was my first top ten record. The more you have accomplished in your career, the easier it is to self-promote. The real trick is when you don't have that depth of experience yet you still need to promote what experience you've got to whatever degree you can to get work.

My friend Waldo [LaTowsky] says that it really comes down to work. All the self-promotion is about making a living playing drums or percussion. It's not about becoming friends and chatting, unless you're talking with people in your own hometown. Make friends that way. If you sign up for all of these groups and have these music industry discussions and stuff, it's only going to take you so far. You can't start globally. You have to start locally. That's why going to Drummer's Lunch is cool. I'm starting to see more guys throwing stuff up on Facebook saying that such and such needs a sub for Milwaukee next week. That's the good thing. That's the good I think social networking will do for work and networking. If they can't do it, they'll help somebody else get it.

Anything you would like to add?

Oh, I don't know. I think I covered a lot of stuff.

There are so many great drummers that have come through this town, and are still coming through every day, like Nick Buda. I met him when he was eighteen years old and he couldn't get a session. Now he's playing with Taylor Swift and a lot of stuff. It's great, but the amount of recording work has shrunk a lot. I don't know the statistics, but I can see that the performance trust fund that comes every August (hopefully it comes today) shows that the amount of total sessions that are being done is going down nationwide.

We used to see million- or two-million-selling records weekly. Now the two artists in a year that sell multiplatinum are more than likely going to be hip-hop or rap, and that will be it. I think the money at the top of the chain that allows recording of songs, records, demos, CDs, you name it—music—that money has become tighter because they aren't seeing a return. People are stealing music left and right. It's just chipped and ate away at the commerce part of the music business to the point where they aren't even getting a return on their investment. So it's better to put it in a bond or a *restaurant* or something.

In the seventies, when I started in Muscle Shoals, there were probably fifteen record labels. Now there are only three majors and the others are subsidiaries. If everything is part of one or two cakes instead of fifteen cakes, then it means there's not going to be that many opportunities to get things out and heard.

So I should have been a teacher because they're rolling in the dough [laughs].

5

TOMMY WELLS

Tommy Wells (June 18, 1951–September 24, 2013) grew up in a musical home and began playing gigs with his father at a very young age. He joined a band with his high school guidance counselor before he was a high school graduate. Some of his earliest recording sessions were in Detroit, "Motown," which was a short drive from his Indiana home. Pressured to attend college by his father, he attended Berklee College of Music in Boston during the week but flew back to Detroit on the weekends to play on recording sessions before he was twenty years old. It is

not surprising that Wells was able to sustain a long musical career, given his pre-Nashville performance success.

His experiences playing in jazz groups, touring in Christian rock bands, and recording R&B songs, television spots, and jingles helped Wells develop a versatility that allowed him to "hit the ground running" when he was given an offer too good to refuse to relocate to Nashville. He quickly made a name for himself recording demos and jingles before becoming firmly established as a first-call drummer for master recording sessions. His list of credits includes work with Don McLean, Foster & Lloyd, Ray Stevens, Ricky Van Shelton, and Charlie Daniels. He recorded a near-countless number of television spots and commercials for such companies as ESPN, McDonald's, and the well-known Taco Bell "Run for the Border" campaign.

Wells passed away in his sleep on September 24, 2013, in Fort Wayne, Indiana, from a brain aneurysm. He was in Fort Wayne for several days of recording sessions at Sweetwater Studios. He and I conducted his interview at Fork's Drum Closet on February 1, 2012. We met there for the first time around ten years earlier. I knew who he was from seeing him play with Jimmy Hall & the Prisoners of Love at 3rd & Lindsley. I struck up a conversation, hoping he would at least give me the opportunity to tell him that I liked his drumming. He sat down on the nearest drum throne and talked to me for over an hour about drumming, advice on how to find work, equipment, and even some of Nashville's drumming history. Similar to our first conversation, this interview details his thoughts and experiences throughout his career, the state of the music industry, and how to build a successful career.

Let's get started with the basics. Where did you grow up?

I grew up all over the Midwest because my dad worked for Dana Holding Corporation, which is a car parts manufacturer. I lived in Michigan, Ohio, and Indiana. I lived in Detroit as a kid for five years. I went to high school in Marion, Indiana.

Did you start playing drums at a young age?

Yeah. There are actually pictures of me playing an old 1890's-era drum, which I still have, when I was, like, eighteen months old. Actually, I played it the other day for the Hunger Beat Down, where a bunch of drummers played Three Camps to raise awareness of world hunger

[January 14, 2012]. That was through an organization called the Global Drummers Alliance. Sam Bacco refurbished the drum.

My dad bought me a set of Rolling Bombers when I was five. They were huge! I got my first modern-day set for Christmas when I was eleven. I think that was in 1962.

Were you taking drum lessons when you were five?

I started lessons when I was eight.

Was that at a music store?

Not at that point. I was in school band. My elementary school band teacher was a drummer named Frank Lane. That was a really good experience because he was a good player. He was one of those teachers that really cared about teaching—and especially the drummers. He offered a little extra help outside band rehearsals.

I got a different drum set when I was eleven. We look back now and realize how cool those Rolling Bomber kits were. At that time, all the guys were playing with twenty-inch bass drums and cool jazz sets even if they were playing rock 'n' roll. I thought the Rolling Bombers were the most uncool things I ever saw. So I got a 1962 Pearl drum set. Jim Pettit from the Memphis Drum Shop has the exact same model in his collection. He's a big-time vintage collector. He's got them in black diamond, just like mine were, in mint condition. I'm jealous.

After that I took lessons from a guy in Detroit named Dennis Dombrowski. He was a local player and did some sessions up there. I studied with him for a couple of years until I moved to Indiana. I lived in Marion, which was about 120 miles south of Elkhart, where Arlene Trafford had Trafford Drum Studio. She was Harold Firestone's sister, who was the rudimental guy.

In high school, I did all the rudimental contest stuff and always did a Firestone solo. I was about as close to the source one could get since Harold was no longer alive. She knew how to play that stuff.

So you had a marching background?

Yeah, the Indiana high school marching band tradition is strong.

Backing up, were you studying the drum set with your first teacher?

Yes, absolutely. He would bring his drums and vibes to the school. We'd work on playing time. He'd play vibes with me. It was interesting because later, when I went to Berklee, I did the same thing with Alan Dawson. I'd play drums while he [Dawson] was working on his vibe stuff.

So you were learning a lot of jazz.

Yeah, my dad was a B-3 player. I grew up with a drum set in the living room next to the B-3 all the time.

Did he have a band?

Well, for a while I was his band. We had other players for a while, but we did gigs as a duo. Sometimes we would play with a guitar player, or as many as a quartet with a horn player who was a local radio personality named Mike Jenkins. It was like that.

My dad taught me some valuable lessons. I'm still working on a couple of those lessons. One of them was, "Shut up and play" [laughs]. He came and watched me one night playing at a Moose Club with a piano trio. I was lucky that we had a family friend named Virginia Long who played piano. It was her band, and I could play underage because they were private clubs. I had all kinds of gigs with her. The bass player was a guy named Gary Phillips, who was my high school counselor. That was funny. I'd get a note during class telling me that I had to report to the office to see my guidance counselor. I'd get out of algebra or something and walk into the office saying, "Hi, Mr. Phillips." He'd reply asking if I was available for a gig on a specific date.

Anyway, my dad came to see me play with them sometimes. Every once in a while, Virginia would call a tune I didn't know, and I'd lean over and ask Gary how it went. He'd say, "It's just a bossa," or whatever. I'd play it, and my dad took me aside and told me not to talk on the bandstand. "If it's a song you don't know, just let the piano player play the intro. You'll know it by letter A. Just shut up and play" [laughs]. I thought that was good advice.

He also used to always tell me to swing harder. I was around fourteen years old playing with my dad at home. We were playing "The Lady Is a Tramp." He stopped and said, "Swing harder," and counted us back in. After about sixteen bars, he stopped again and said, "Don't rush. Just swing harder." So he began to tell me to look at him when he was playing a bossa or rock tune. He was sitting straight up. Then he told me to watch him when playing a Miles [Davis] tune like "Milestones"; he was all hunched over and digging in. He said, "See how much harder that swings?" So there you go. I learned a lot about body language and how that communicates to an audience. The way you feel is the way you play. That's how I learned how to swing harder [laughs].

You've talked a lot about playing jazz. Obviously, Detroit is well known for its R&B tradition. Were you doing much of that?

Yes. Of course, when I was in high school, I lived in Indiana. However, the closest real recording studios were in Detroit. I started to work in Detroit in the summer of 1969 when I turned eighteen, and some people that I knew in Indiana went there to record some stuff. Through that work, I met some people at United Sound Systems, which was the oldest studio in Detroit. There was another place called the Funk Factory where I worked, as well as Sound Pattern, which was owned by an engineer that had worked at Motown named Danny Dallas.

I was a kid and these guys liked me and the way I played. I went to Berklee in September 1969. My dad wanted me to go to college. That's pretty much the only reason I went to music school. I was getting these calls to go back to Detroit for things that people I knew were doing, like the soundtracks for *Wild World of Sports*, almost every week. We were mostly doing content and background music with some solo songs, like "Jean-Claude What's-His-Name?" about Jean-Claude Killy, who was used on broadcasts.

There was an airline, Mohawk Airlines, which flew prop planes from Detroit to Boston. A one-way ticket was thirty-five dollars. I would get done with school on Friday afternoon, go the airport, and fly to Detroit for thirty-five bucks. I'd track on Saturday and Sunday, head to the airport, and catch the last flight to Boston on Sunday night. It was funny because my teachers at school, Fred Buda (who I could talk about for an hour) and Alan Dawson, sat me down and asked what I was doing there. I said, "Well, my dad wanted me to go to college. This seemed like the best place because I really want to play." Buda said, "Everybody here wants to graduate and do what you're already doing. You can always come back." I said, "Would you tell my dad that?" He said he would. They called my dad—I was in the room—and talked to him. December 5, 1969, was my last day at Berklee.

I went back to Detroit, started recording a lot, and joined a band called Dust. The band got a record deal. I went from that band to a band called First Gear with Larnelle Harris. Working with those bands got me a lot of work because the rhythm section was used regularly to play on other records.

I'm going to back things up a little bit before we get too far away—Fred Buda . . .

Yes! He was great! The most important thing that I learned from Fred was physical. He was into the Moeller stroke stuff and ergonomics, much like Freddie Gruber. The first thing he showed me when I was there was how to change my grip. I'm forever grateful for that. The first thing he did was set a person down at the drum set and have them play some time. Of course, I was as nervous as could be. About ten seconds in, he grabs my shoulders and says, "Relax!"

He made sure that my drums were set up in a way that didn't restrict my movement. He had me move my floor tom out so my arm didn't get constricted when I moved in that direction. It should be comfortable. He had me position my snare drum so that when I dropped my arm to a playing position, the stick naturally rested in the middle of the drum. My legs are just above parallel because of the height of my drum throne. Everything is set up in such a way that I can reach everything without having to add tension to that limb. Things like that have really helped me play pain free for my entire career. I'm almost sixty-one years old. There are other players my age and a lot of them are playing hurt—big names in the drumming industry even. I don't want to name names, but they have repetitive motion injuries, carpal tunnel; another guy has a degenerative nerve situation. Most of that stems from spending so many hours at the drums, as session players do all day and night, playing in a manner that put unnecessary stress on the body. I've never had any of those problems because of Fred. I guess that's luck that he was my teacher, but it sure did work out for me.

And you studied with Alan Dawson too.

Yeah. The thing that I did with Alan was play. He played vibraphone and I played drums. A lot of times there was a bass player named Major Holley. He was an old swing-era player. He was a funny cat and a really great player. I played with those guys in Alan's teaching room. I learned all about playing time and styles. I had never heard of a *nañigo* before. He taught me those kinds of things, and it was just so we could play together.

I took more lessons with them than I was supposed to. I was only supposed to have one lesson a week, but I'd see Fred on his breaks three or four days a week. I'd see Alan every day. I had a lesson with Fred on Monday, and then Alan would be on his break for thirty minutes when I finished with Fred. He'd be getting a Coke, drinking coffee, or playing vibes. So my second week, Alan stopped me and said, "Man, you sound pretty good. Do you want to play?" Um, sure [laughs]. Who wouldn't take him up on that? He wasn't actually supposed to be my teacher. It just kind of happened. I'd see him, sometimes, five days a week. I'd go over to his office at four in the afternoon to play for thirty minutes. Major Holley was two doors down, and he'd come over to sit in with us if he was free. It was great. We'd just call tunes and play.

And you were flying to Detroit for sessions on the weekends.
Yeah.

Did you ever get into a situation in Detroit where some of the things that you were learning at Berklee didn't fit? Did you ever become the overplaying music student?
No, not really. I just knew when I was playing R&B, rock, or the *Wide World of Sports* stuff in Detroit that I just had to play the song. If you played too much, somebody would just say, "You know what? Just play it right, okay?"

In high school and after Berklee, I played with a lot of the local jazz guys. There was a pianist named Bill Kennaugh in Indianapolis who I worked with from around the time I was fifteen years old until I left for Nashville, and he's still playing up there. He's a great pianist and arranger. I also worked with Al Kiger and Wayne Darling up there. Wayne taught at North Texas State University after that. This was right around 1970. My jazz days pretty much ended there because my work in Detroit led to my playing with First Gear. That was a horn band. We opened up into some jazzy things, but it was a horn rock band.

Your first band was Dust. What was that band like?
That was a rock band. We did one record. We did a lot of high school assemblies and college concert tours. Those tours were set up with assemblies during the day and a concert every night at either a high school or college. They were booked for free with the assembly show, which included some sort of positive message like responsibility or anti-drug. At night, we did a traditional show. We did assemblies five days a

week during the day and then played full concerts six nights a week. We would have a Sunday afternoon show every once in a while too.

Was Dust signed to a label?

Yes. They were on the Young America Showcase and then Myrrh, which was a Christian label. I left Dust to play with First Gear. Larnelle Harris is still a gospel artist to this day. Those were beginnings as well. That band was pretty much the same deal as Dust—assemblies and such. I worked on stuff in Detroit when we weren't out, but we were out a lot.

We did two albums with First Gear. I left that band to play with Dust for another year because the music industry basically left Detroit in 1972 when Motown shut down. It eventually died, and I was in Nashville by 1975.

In those days, I wasn't a full-time session drummer. I was more of a part-time session drummer and full-time on the road.

I came here [Nashville] to play with a guy named Gene Cotton, who was having hits. He was on ABC Records when I got here. I met him all the way back in 1970. I ran across him in Indiana at Anderson College. We got along really well. When it was time for him to hire a full-time band, he decided to bring me to Nashville.

It was literally the gig that you can't refuse because he built a two-story building on the alley on Beechwood just a few blocks from here [Fork's Drum Closet]. There is a huge house at 1712 Beechwood that we lived in at the time. The bottom of the building was a rehearsal studio and his photography studio. There was an apartment upstairs that was brand new.

We saw each other at a show in Florida. He took me out to Denny's in Lake Wales, Florida. He said, "Here's the deal: I want you to come to Nashville. You put your drums in the rehearsal studio. You can play whenever you want. You can live upstairs. I'm going to pay you a retainer every week, x amount per show, and x amount per diem." He just laid it all out there and said, "What do you say?" I told him I'd be there in two weeks. I had to give notice and get somebody to take my place in Dust. That's how it happened.

Larrie Londin really helped me get around when I got here. I tagged along with him to watch him do sessions. That experience taught me how to handle myself when I started getting calls. I met him in Michigan when I was twelve years old. My dad took me to the Rooster Tail in downtown Detroit. He [Larrie] was probably seventeen at the time, and we kept in touch over the years.

I saw him again when I was with Dust and we recorded a record in Nashville with a producer named Robert John Gallo. Larrie was booked to play percussion on the sessions for three days. He played tambourines, congas, and shakers here and there. At the end of the session, he took me aside and said, "You know why I was here?" I said, "Yeah, to play percussion." He said, "Well, I was hired to make sure you could cut it and to be ready to play drums if you couldn't handle it" [laughs]. No pressure. It's a good thing I didn't know why he was hired.

He and I became friends at that time. I mean, good enough friends that I flew to Nashville on Sundays, on travel days with Dust, before I moved here. I'd go to his house and play drums all day. We'd hang, set up two sets of drums, and play along with records until it was time to call it a night. I'd sleep at his place, and he'd drop me off at the airport on Monday morning while he was on his way to his session. We did that, and then I moved here.

Basically, I learned about the chart system. I don't mean just the Nashville Number System. Larrie had his own way of charting out songs that he taught me. I still use it to this day. Kroon and I taught at the Nashville Session Drummers Workout eleven or twelve years ago to about fifty students, including guys like Rich Redmond, Chris Brown, Brian Pruitt, Billy Mason—they all did the class with us. Some of them went on to do real well. Anyway, this charting that Kroon and I use just uses the number *1* instead of chord changes written in phrase lengths. There's shorthand where you circle things to put figures in. Check marks and brackets mean different things. It's handy because it allows you to look at a chart and see all the phrases, punches, and figures in one glance so you're not locked to a chart.

I learned about reading the Nashville Numbers from him, of course. I'm sure you know that Larrie changed the way that drums are played in country music. I mean that literally—the entire approach. Before Londin, you had Buddy Harman and Kenny Buttrey to some extent. Buttrey played on a lot of the rock stuff, like Bob Dylan. He played like a rock drummer even with Jimmy Buffett.

Of course, everybody knows Buddy Harman invented the stick-and-brush thing. He brought drums to country music and played on some great rock records, like the Everly Brothers, Roy Orbison—"Pretty

Woman" and "Only the Lonely." When Larrie came in, the first thing he cut was the Jerry Reed stuff, like "Amos Moses" and "When You're Hot, You're Hot." That had a whole different feel to it instead of the straight up and down, *boom, chick, boom, chick.* It was cut in half. It still had the straight up-and-down thing, which had been heard for years. He was playing straight fours on the kick, with the snare drum and hi-hat in half-time, which Larrie called "The Blue Beat." He also did the "Three-Legged Dog" [Wells sings]:

He did all of this stuff and had names for it that people would remember. I think Porter Wagoner actually came up with some of these names, and Larrie just kept them. They were his grooves, but it changed the way drums were played in country music. If you listen to Porter Wagoner, Dolly Parton, or Jerry Reed from that era—there was nothing like that before.

Another thing: Pearl drums had the fiberglass concert toms that were real similar to the [Allen F.] Blaemire concert toms that Hal Blaine was using in Los Angeles. Larrie brought that to Nashville. That kind of became the norm after him. Jerry Carrigan and Jerry Kroon began using them, which really went a long way to making that the Nashville drum sound. Along with that, there was the real tight bass drum and big, fat snare drum. This was the 1970s. You would very consistently see eight- and ten-inch toms on a stand, two concert toms on the bass drum, and at least one on the floor. Larrie played that way with eight- and ten-inch toms on a stand, twelve- and thirteen-inch toms on the bass drum, and fourteen- and sixteen-inch toms on the floor.

Six toms?

Yeah, then he cut it down to the even numbers—eight, ten, twelve, fourteen, and sixteen. He took what Hal [Blaine] and John Guerin were doing in Los Angeles and made it fit in Nashville. Beyond that, there were a lot of rock acts that Larrie played with—especially Canadian rock acts. He played that setup with those groups.

Were those Canadian acts coming to Nashville to record?

Yeah. Robert Gallo was producing a lot of that [laughs]. So you can see how a lot of this ties together. As a matter of fact, I believe Larrie used that setup on a Steve Perry record—the fiberglass toms.

Let's talk about your setup. What did you bring to Nashville?

Early on I was playing a standard kit. I had different drum sets for different tours. I was doing so many shows with those heavy touring groups that the drums would just get killed after a year.

Did you have a brand you stuck with?

I played Ludwigs the first year out. I bought a Rogers set. That kit broke down a lot because of the Swiv-O's [tom mount], so I sent that kit home. We were in California, and we did some tracking for First Gear at a place called MCA-Whitney in Glendale. I saw Hal Blaine in one room, and we were in the other. He had his Blaemire concert toms with him. I went over and talked to him. "Mr. Blaine, what are these drums?" He let me play them, and I liked them. This was about July 1972. I had my Rogers kit, and loved it, but the Swiv-O's were getting wonky. I was carrying all of these extra parts. That was getting old.

I walked into a place in St. Louis called Reno Drums owned by a guy named Jack Reno. He had a set of used burgundy sparkle Blaemire drums. It had two twenty-inch kicks, and twelve-, fourteen-, sixteen-, and eighteen-inch toms. I bought the kit for $250. It's funny because he included packing up my Rogers kit and sending it to my parents' Detroit house in the price [laughs]. It was a great deal. I played them on the road.

I got my Pearl deal and sent my Blaemire drums to Detroit in late 1972. That was with Walt Johnston from Pearl, who I met through Larrie Londin, and Neal Graham, who had XL Percussion for years and is now with Gator Cases. They set it up so that my drums came to Neal, and I picked them up with the cases. I got a wood/fiberglass set and a fiberglass set with the concert toms.

The Blaemires became my session kit because my Pearl drums were always on the truck. I sold the Blaemires later for, like, two hundred dollars in around 1975 because I didn't have anywhere to keep them. That was before I moved to Nashville. If you ever see a burgundy sparkle Blaemire kit, I want them back. Speaking of setups, Neal found me eight- and ten-inch bare fiberglass toms to go with that kit soon after I got them. So be on the lookout if they ever show up on eBay [laughs].

I was with Pearl until 1986. I signed with Remo and played those drums for ten years. They trimmed their artist roster except for Jeff Hamilton. I've been playing Gretsch now for eleven years. I've always had a set of Gretsch toms—from about 1976 and on. Some people just like the Gretsch tom sound. If a producer asks for Gretsch toms, you take them with you.

I had a guy that always requested DW bass drums. I've always had a DW shell, even when I was with Remo, to make him happy. It looked like a Remo drum, but it had a DW shell underneath. You have to find ways to keep everybody happy [laughs].

You moved to Nashville with the Gene Cotton gig. How did you branch out from that?

I was fortunate that the other people in the band were getting session calls. They were recommending me for work. The fact that I had been doing it in Detroit gave me a bit of street credibility.

But you had examples of records that you had played on up there.

Yeah, there was First Gear and Dust plus some other things. Most of it you wouldn't know much about unless you were into the Christian rock scene, like Bloody Truth, Crimson Bridge, or Pilgrim 20. In 1973 or 1974, we did a lot of what would be referred to as club or disco records. There would be an entire side of a vinyl twelve-inch record with seventeen or twenty minutes filled with one instrumental piece. A lot of that stuff was cut with a full rhythm section and horns, with everything in the same room, to eight-track at the Funk Factory in Detroit.

It was around 1974, we were playing in Florida on Saturday night and I had a session in Detroit on Monday morning. We got done and I started driving at about ten p.m. I drove straight through to Detroit right to the studio. Danny Dallas let me in. I went to the drum room, took the blanket out of the bass drum, and slept until it was time to work. Danny woke me up with enough time for me to go to the bathroom to clean up and hit the downbeat [laughs]. I wanted to play on records, so I had to do whatever I could to make it happen, right?

So recording was something that you got a taste for in Detroit and didn't want to let go of, right?

Right. Even though I moved to Nashville to play with Gene, I knew that Larrie was here and that I was going to get a shot. I did. I started playing on Gene's records, and that led me to playing on other people's records. I started doing demos for the guys in the band. That was easy to do back in the day.

And that was a lot of country music?

I learned how to play country, initially, from Larrie. I went and watched Buddy Harman too. He is a very nice man. People like to say that this person or that person is the most recorded drummer in history, but I think the facts show that Buddy Harman owns that title.

You think so.

Absolutely, especially according to the number of sessions played. I've seen it written down because the union wrote it out for him. It was more than Hal. Hal and Buddy did a thing at the NAMM Show here probably eleven or twelve years ago. Buddy shared the amount of sessions he played. You have to remember, they [the "A Team"] were doing four sessions a day at ten a.m., two p.m., six p.m, and ten p.m. in their heyday, more than five days a week. There were acts that would wait until they could get a certain combination of players together, and if that meant working on Sunday, then they were working on Sunday. They were just hitting it.

They were playing on country, pop, and rock records. It was an astronomical number of sessions.

Do you think the number is in the tens of thousands?

Yeah. When you think of playing four sessions a day mostly six days a week from the mid-1950s until the mid-1970s, that's an unbelievable amount of sessions. They were recording everything. Like I said, there was country, rock, pop, easy listening . . . the list goes on. Buddy was friends with Hal. They went to Roy Knapp's school in Chicago together when they got out of the service. This is obviously before they did what they did. Hal went to L.A. and played on everything [laughs] in the 1960s, and Buddy came here and did the same thing from the mid-1950s through the mid-1970s.

And you were spending time with Buddy and Larrie when you first moved here.

Buddy was a really nice guy too. He ended up working for the union later. Before that, I saw him do a lot of the stick-and-brush thing, and the thing with the upright bass where he only played the kick on the downbeat of the chorus. Larrie was the opposite end of the spectrum who was just slamming with that hard four-on-the-floor. I wanted to learn all of it so I could be ready for any situation, especially if I'm asked to play like either of those two, which still happens. If I'm asked to play a "Ray Price" shuffle, I mean, I saw Buddy do it. I just try to do exactly what he did.

He played on all of the Patsy Cline records. People sometimes say, "Oh, Buddy, yeah, the stick-and-brush thing . . . ," but he had chops. If you want to hear that, listen to the Patsy Cline record called "Strange." I play that song in a show called *Country Royalty* and had to re-record that for a CD that goes with it. I remember listening to it and thinking, "You know what? Give me about five minutes because I've got to work that up." It's almost a Latin-feel with brushes, and it's based on five- and seven-stroke rolls. You can tell that Buddy could do more than play simple time when you listen to records like that.

Of course, Larrie could play. He was always working hard on his chops. He had a great feel and a lot of power. He played what was required for the record, which didn't always require great hands. He was working on his hands from the early 1970s, and he figured it out, man. He had great chops! When he started doing drum clinics, he really had it together. You have to give him credit. He was already successful playing on tons of hit records. Nobody had a better feel than he did, and he was always working on new things.

I learned a lot from him, and a lot of it didn't have anything to do with playing the drums. He understood that you have to be your own best salesman. When he went to work, he had the personality and confidence to make things happen. You could tell that everybody knew that it was going to be great if he was there. He understood that. I don't want to say he had a knack for that, but he knew how to behave and make you feel confident in him.

I've always been kind of, I don't like to say this, but shy. I'm not very outgoing. That isn't my natural personality, and he was larger than life. I did learn that you make sure everybody feels welcome—not alienated.

You're going to be spending a lot of hours with people on some long days. Learn to care about these people, and not just as guys you're playing with for a few days. As it turns out, almost all of my friends are session players because I've spent a great part of my life with them. I saw Larrie be that way with people, and you couldn't help but notice and understand it. It's not just about being a great musician, but working together well because they get along. You become like brothers.

For me, especially with some of the bass players, it's like seeing a brother when you see them. I might not see somebody for weeks, but it's like a reunion when we get together. It's that much of a relationship. Making music is just another part of it.

Jerry Kroon is another guy worth mentioning. I don't think he gets as much recognition as the other guys. He played on a *ton* of records. He's a great guy with a whole different personality than Larrie or Eddie [Bayers Jr.], who are great with people. People call Jerry "The Hammer" or "Ol' Country Jerr." People respect him, and he has a lot of friends that are session players. You always know where you stand with Jerry.

They had a piece of [two-inch] tape out at Chelsea Recording Studio for a while where you could hear Jerry count off a song, play about eight bars, and then you hear a loud *wham!* on the drums where he throws his sticks down, the drum room opens, and Jerry says, "You can't rock if you can't lock!" [laughs]. And then the drum room door slams again. You knew where you stood with him [laughs]. He's one of my best friends and has been for years.

He and I do things that are unrelated to music. We go to hockey games and stuff. He's been with Don McLean for fourteen years or so. That's his live gig. They'll do some dates in Europe and Australia. You can see Jerry on the Don McLean PBS special with Garth Brooks singing "American Pie." He's playing and *killing!* He says he's retired, but not really. He's out there working still.

Let's get back to you. We were talking about your start in Nashville. Where were some of the places you were working when you were getting started?

I did work at Silverline/Goldline. That was owned by Roy Clark and the Oak Ridge Boys. There was a producer named Noel Fox there. There was a place called Sawgrass Music, which was a publishing company. Jimmy Darrell was producing there.

The first big deal that I got when I started working all the time was playing at Tree, which eventually became Sony Tree. It was Buddy Killen's publishing house. They had a lot of writers, like Harlan Howard, Curly Putman, and a lot of the old school guys were signed there, which led to him signing a lot of the younger writers too. The studio at Tree was, and still is, a very good place.

You could do demos that would turn into master recordings. Sometimes people would hear a demo in the right key for the artist and just buy the track. The quality was good enough that they were being used on the final product. I've had that happen from demos at Tree as recently as 2011. I actually had a demo we did for Gretchen Peters turn into a master just last year. We probably recorded that on the same session we did the demo for Martina McBride's "Independence Day." That was cut with Gretchen, so it was, what, twenty years ago?

They had great engineers working at Tree on days they weren't cutting big records. That was great. I would work there four or five days a week if I had the openings.

So you got a lot of work in Nashville pretty quickly.

Yeah, this was in the late seventies. I was working at Tree, Silverline, and Sawgrass. I was also picking up work at Warner Brothers and MCA. You have to understand, there were more demos in those days and less players. Demos paid forty dollars a session up until 1992.

When Paul Overstreet first came in and signed with Silverline, we did his first sessions at ten, two, six, and ten. We probably did four or five songs per session. I made $160 working all day—and that was before taxes. Those were pretty long days. So, you think, we were losing taxes and fees. It wasn't a lot of money. It was probably a hundred dollars per day when it was all said and done, but it was great.

We approached making demos the same way we did when we were doing a record. Everybody that was doing demos out of the twenty or twenty-five that I was working with were also cutting records. Nobody ever thought they were doing work that was beneath them. Some of the guys in that group were Bobby Ogden or Shane Keister on piano, Sonny Garrish was playing steel—let me say something about him.

I still work with him [Sonny Garrish] these days. I reminded him of something that he taught me. We would be in the control room listening to the pre-production demo before cutting the demo. He would be writing all over his chart—just everywhere. I said, "Man, I can't believe how much you write on your charts." He said, "Take care of your chart and your chart will take care of you." It's true. That's when I started writing every little thing on my chart. It cuts down on the amount of times you have to re-record something because you forgot some little detail. Just play the chart and you'll be in good shape.

So I was playing on Gene Cotton's records and doing some Christian rock records too. I was working with Patty Roberts and some other records that had big production. That was all going on at the same time.

Correct me if I'm wrong, but didn't you join a band in the early 1980s?

I did. I joined a band called RPM with some really talented people.

The band history acknowledges that you were already a well-known session drummer before joining.

That's right. Brent Maher was producing them, and I knew him real well from doing Gene Cotton's records, among other things. He had me come in and play on it. Joe English played on some of it before I got there. None of that came out. The drums were great, but they hadn't really found their identity yet. No fault of his.

The first thing we recorded ended up being the first single from the first record from the demo. They kind of found their identity. We did that at Creative Workshop. The session where I came in was the one where they hit on their sound. It was fortunate for me that I was there when it all came together. I'd like to take credit for that, but I don't think I can [laughs]. I was there, we ran the songs down, and it worked.

So we did that record for Brent Maher for EMI Records. The group left EMI and went to Warner Brothers. The second record was recorded in London at SARM West, which is owned by Trevor Horn. I went over there and was there for almost two months. The band were the coproducers with Gary Langan.

I was in that band until February 1985, when they decided they were going to move to Los Angeles. I didn't even consider moving with them.

Were they a very popular band?

There was some success. We had a top five record in Texas. The station KLOL in Houston wanted us to headline their summer festival. We did a few small gigs around here [Nashville] and headlined the summer fest at the Astrodome [laughs]. That was hard to top.

The record did well and got good airplay. There were some places throughout the country where we hit like that. The second album did okay. We did *Solid Gold* and some other TV. They wanted to move before the third album. As it turns out, they all ended up moving back here. I was playing on enough records by then that I wasn't interested in being in any more bands.

Were you brought in as a band member or playing as a sideman?

I was a band member.

Did being in a band have any impact on your session work?

The only time it was affected was when I went to England. Other than that, it was largely a recording project that didn't do that many dates. My session work was really gaining momentum during that time. I think, maybe in some ways, being in RPM helped me get some sessions because country was getting a little more rock flavored and people heard me doing that. It probably at least got me the first shot at some things.

I was doing some records with Holly Dunn, Mike Martin-Murphy, and even Kathy Mattea's first record had some rock vibe to them. I recorded Jo-El Sonnier's "Tear Stained Letter" and "Crazy Over You" with Foster & Lloyd. Those are pretty rockin' for country. Both Foster & Lloyd records rocked pretty hard. Jo-El's first record was the same. I'm not sure why I got the call for that stuff, but playing with RPM probably opened the door. I think I was considered a rock guy that could play on country records for a lot of years. Now I'm probably just considered a country guy. Who knows?

I think of myself, more than anything, as an R&B drummer. My Detroit roots are always there. I play in a band now called the Detroit/ Memphis Experience with Tim & Roddy Smith, who you know real well. Darryl Johnson is in the band, and he sang with a bunch of different people, including Chairmen of the Board. A lot of it is original music in that classical R&B style, and it feels like going home for me. I think that style is the most comfortable for me as a player.

Back to the 1980s, you mentioned some records that you played on, but you were also doing jingle work.

That's when the jingle work in Nashville really exploded. It carried through into the mid-1990s. We did everything you can think of. We did Taco Bell "Run for the Border" and the Budweiser stuff with Hank

Jr. Almost all of the country acts did some beer ad. The Texas acts did the Lonestar Beer spots. We did all of that and Coke, Pepsi, McDonald's. We were recording a lot of jingles.

How challenging was that?

It depends on the needs of the day.

Let me elaborate. I've always heard stories about ridiculous meter changes in the songs to line up with cuts in the video and such. Did you experience much of that?

There was a lot of that. I didn't have trouble with that. You just have to play it like that's the way it's supposed to be. If you listen to it, most people don't pick up on it. I just blasted through them, and it made all the timings come out. The drum machine allowed us to do some different things. We could adjust the tempo by a beat or two, and take one of those odd bars out. I got to the point where I would be sitting there with my calculator [to calculate beats-per-minute timing differences] and drum machine, and I'd say, "This doesn't feel that bad if we play it two clicks faster. If we do that, we can add one beat back in and it works out." Nashville is great like that because players can make recommendations like that. Then we'd see how it would go, and it would work.

Did you watch the video while you were playing?

Usually, no. Very often for TV spots, we'd watch the video and then go in and play. Then they'd sync it up and we'd watch it back. A lot of the time they wouldn't have video. There were also radio spots.

Doing jingles is fun. Mike Stewart, who is one of the jingle producers at Dan Williams Music, said, and this is the truth, that "the jingle is an 'a la' business." What does that mean? "Can you do this song a la the Rolling Stones? Can you do this a la the Beatles? Or Van Halen?" People from the ad agency, the company, and jingle producer are at the session. They all have their own ideas what they want a spot to be, and all of their ideas are based on something that was on the radio at the time.

Of course, when T. Graham Brown got involved with Taco Bell, we had to do everything like his stuff. We would play just like his records. He had a bunch of big country hits in the 1980s, like "Hell or High Water" and "Darlene." He did all of the "Run for the Border" stuff. He sang on it and was in the video spots. There's video with T. and Little Richard together.

The thing about jingles was, and we talked about this earlier, that I could look at my schedule and see if I was light on master recordings or demos. If that was the case, I would just say, "Well, I guess this is a jingle week." The jingle guys get stuff approved and they want to record the next day. Sunday night the phone would ring, and Monday was the session. That was normal. It was either for Dan Williams Music, Hummingbird Music, or Ron Chancey Productions. Those three companies were working all the time for seventeen or eighteen years.

There were some funny times then. I would work all day for Dan Williams recording McDonald's spots, and then have a six o'clock for Ron Chancey at Woodland Studios, and it would be another McDonald's spot. They were recording so many things that they were using multiple jingle companies, doing separate campaigns at the same time. It was a lot of work that was usually fun.

The only time it wasn't fun was when there were too many ad agency and corporate people there. They didn't know what they were doing, but they knew what they wanted. They didn't know how to tell you. It could get crazy. You'd have five people telling the musicians what to do. Then you would do it ten different ways before the jingle producer would say, "Okay, we've had our fun. I'm going to record the spot." Then we'd get it done, and all of the ad agency and corporate guys would be in the control room smiling. But we had to play the game every once in a while. Sometimes you can't go directly from A to B. Every once in a while it's all the way to Z and then back around [laughs].

Are there any records that you played on that you're particularly proud of?

I'm proud of anything that did well because that means somebody liked it. The country stuff is probably what most people have heard that I've done. I'd say Ricky Van Shelton's stuff, like "Crime of Passion," "Life Turned Her That Way," or "Life's Little Ups and Downs." I thought we made really good records, and he was a really great singer.

I'm really proud of the first two Foster & Lloyd records. It's the first time that a group's first single went to number one in country. That was "Crazy Over You." That was different than anything prior to that. I played a piccolo snare on "Crime of Passion" with Ricky maybe ten days before "Crazy Over You." I carried that drum around, and nobody would let me play it on anything. Then I played it on those two records and they both went to number one. I played that snare drum a lot for the next few years because a lot of people wanted that sound.

It's funny. Kenny Malone mentioned that deep field drums were the go-to instrument for a long time.

They were. Larrie started that. He played a six- or eight-inch-deep snare drum. He had a ten-by-fourteen-inch snare drum that was a Pearl phenolic shell drum. That was a synthetic material that they made marching drums out of at the time. He had one, so we all had to have one [laughs]. Larrie played that drum on the England Dan & John Ford Coley records. Some of the 1970s pop stuff is that drum—check out "Nights Are Forever Without You"

I think Kenny Malone got his from Larrie, who was kind of selling Pearl stuff out of his house at the time. I bought one from Larrie in '73 or so. I have a Canadian album that Larrie did around 1972 with Dwayne Ford where he definitely used it.

They only worked when you had an engineer that knew how to record it using two microphones. A drum that deep with a Shure SM57 on top doesn't work because it's too far away from the snares on the bottom. You get too many high frequencies that way. The analog EQs in those days had noise in the high frequencies. Some engineers like Brent Maher and some others knew how to make that drum sound good with two microphones and the phase reversed on the bottom mic. That's basic stuff that we think of now.

When I played the piccolo on the Foster & Lloyd and Ricky Van Shelton things, it had such a "crack" to it. I played that drum a lot and things started to go in that direction. The other guys began doing that too. Those were the first records that had that sound.

I'm glad we're talking about gear. I want to say for the record that you are respected as one of the foremost experts on drums and equipment by your peers. How have you been able to keep up with the amount of information that is out there over the years?

[laughs] I'm fortunate to be able to do something that I love. I not only love playing the drums, but I really like the drums as an instrument. If you go online, you'll find me on Drum Forum and Press Roll. Tonight, when I'm not working, I'll go and snoop around. It's very interesting to me. There's always been somebody around that knows a

lot about drums, and I enjoy picking their brain. Clay Fuqua, who is the drum repair guy here at Fork's Drum Closet, and Sam Bacco are real knowledgeable about vintage drums. If you want to know something about an old Ludwig, vintage stuff, or years, Clay knows that stuff. He's also very connected in that world.

For example, think about piccolo snare drums. I always liked the sound of them. Stewart Copeland was playing them in the late 1970s. It wasn't a piccolo drum, but it was a Ludwig Supraphonic cranked up. Then the piccolo came out. They are so great because the snares are so close to the mic. It's easier to get that sound for engineers. It's instant before they even EQ it or anything. That isn't popular right now. We're back to playing deeper drums like the six-and-a-half-inch depth. The piccolo came and went just like the big, fat sound did. Now we're in the middle somewhere. Most six-and-a-half-inch-deep drums will have two mics on them. Things change, and that's really interesting to me.

You're also drawn to electronics too.

Well, yeah. That's something that Larrie got started. He made it so that everybody had to do it. I just thought, "If we're going to do this, I'm going to do it right." Producers will know that I'll be able to do that when they call me. I used to have a twenty-four-space rack, ddrums, Simmons, an Akai sampler, a sixteen-channel Hill mixer with a trigger cleaner to clean up the signal before it got to the electronics. The ddrum3 built a trigger cleaner into the box. A trigger is just a cheap microphone on a drum really. We had all that stuff.

You don't need as much stuff anymore. You can run a loop from a drum machine or laptop. Triggering can be done so much more efficiently in a DAW using sound replacement like Drumagog. There are programs that will have the samples included, and they sound really good. If somebody wants to do replacement or enhancements with samples, it's better to do it in a computer versus using a box that is trying to read a trigger signal off a drum and convert it to MIDI. That way only has a dynamic range of forty decibels, which is really limiting, versus the dynamic range of an acoustic drum set. The DAW will track your performance much more accurately with a 120-decibel dynamic range. They will also trigger different samples for different dynamic ranges to match the different characteristics of striking a drum at higher velocities. The old way is obsolete. I haven't done it the old way in over ten years.

We pretty much skipped talking about the 1990s.

For me, the nineties were just doing the next record with a lot of acts like Ricky Van Shelton, Foster & Lloyd, and Jo-El Sonnier. I was doing a lot of jingles, until they started to go away in the latter part of the decade. I probably haven't done a jingle in a year.

You do a lot of soundalike stuff, right?

Yes. For a while I was working with three different companies, but I am now just with one. That part of the business has changed as well. The company I work for now sells the tracks overseas so other artists can do them in their home countries in their language. They'll also use them as karaoke tracks in the United States.

I was doing rock and country soundalikes until about a year ago. Now it's predominantly country. That's okay with me because the rock stuff was very time consuming. Some of the timing of the double bass stuff on some of the alternative rock took a lot of effort. I figured out that I was working for about a dollar an hour by the time we charted it all out, worked it up, and then tracked it. The country stuff, even though it can be pretty complex because I'll have to re-create the loop, is a lot like playing rock music from ten years ago. Doing twenty of those a month is enough work to keep me busy. I've got ten to do on Monday, so I'll start working on those this afternoon.

Do you record them at home?

No, but I'll do my homework in advance so things go smoothly. I'll transcribe everything so I play them note for note. The goal is to start at nine a.m. on Monday and be finished with ten songs by two p.m. That will include, for me, any of the percussion overdubs. There were two or three songs last week where I had to do four or five percussion passes, plus the drum set track—congas, tambourine, fills with timbales, shaker, and other stuff. That gives us about thirty minutes per song.

It depends, you know. Some records have no percussion and some have a ton. And you know what? It's easy to tell who's playing percussion on the records with a lot of percussion: it's Tom Roady. I can tell when he goes in. He plays real shakers and tambourines, plus the Roland HandSonic. When I hear that, I smile and go, "Here's Roady." He knew what to do on a record. He could do just one little thing that made the song so much better. He was great at filling up the "islandy" stuff. So just last week I was recreating his parts. They were great.

How have you seen the business change over the last thirty or forty years?

Boy, it's changed in a lot of different ways from when I first broke in and people were buying vinyl records. It went from being R&B and rock groups to disco. A lot of sessions were created by disco because the drum machines weren't capable. The disco records in the 1970s, the club records, twelve-inch vinyl records, all have beats per minute on them so the DJs could synchronize them and go from one turntable to the next.

I can tell you how we did that in Detroit: the Seth Thomas Windup Metronome in the closet with a microphone on it. The second engineer had to take care of it. He'd have to wind it. A lot of times, the beats per minute would be accurate for the first two or three minutes. After that, they'd just duck it in the mix because they knew the metronome was going to run out. We would be freewheeling until the end. It might speed up a few clicks. So the beats per minute would be accurate at the beginning of the song when the needle was dropped, but not at the end.

For me, coming to Nashville, country music was in the "country-politan" era in the 1970s. There were acts like Barbara Mandrell. There were strings and not so hardcore country. It went more traditional a little bit before Foster & Lloyd, Jo-El, and Ricky Van Shelton brought in the rockabilly thing in the mid-1980s. After that, Garth Brooks showed up and it turned into "hat" acts with him, Alan Jackson, and those kinds of guys.

Of course, things really changed in the mid- to late 1990s when the illegal downloads started. That's been the biggest change in the music business. You look around and there's a whole generation of people that have probably never bought music in their lives. You talk to high school kids, which I've done because I've been a hockey coach to that age group for a long time, and they all have iPods. I'll ask, "How many songs do you have on your iPod?" It could be anywhere from one hundred to thousands. "How many of those did you buy?" "Psh."

The only time that generation buys music is if they get a gift card. Then they'll use it. They see no reason why they should have to spend money on music when it's there for free. And they *love* music, but spending money on it is absurd to them. That money is for gas, taking their girlfriends to the movies, or buying new hockey equipment. That has had a huge effect on the music business and its contraction.

It's also made record deals different. The "360 record deal" came out of that. When an artist signs a new deal, they will have to give up almost everything, because the record company isn't going to recoup their investment unless it's Taylor Swift or somebody huge like that. Record budgets are much lower. There's another part that I'll come back to. Record budgets are lower; artists are giving up a piece of every revenue stream they will create for the duration of the contract so the company can recoup the recording and promotion budgets. Every concert they do, every TV performance, and *anything* . . . part of it goes back to the record company.

The 360 contract started with Simon Cowell. To get on the TV portion of *American Idol*, an aspiring artist has to sign a 360 deal with Simon Cowell. *American Idol* gets a piece of everything the artist makes for the duration of the contract. Once that happened, it was adopted by the whole recording industry.

The part I wanted to come back around to: because budgets have gotten lower, the American Federation of Musicians came up with a new pay scale called the low-budget scale. On any record that has a budget of a hundred thousand dollars or less, which is most of them now, they don't have to pay full scale. So you hear about "double scale." There's more being done that not only isn't double scale but is paying at two-thirds of single master scale. A three-hour master scale session pays around $360, so low budget is around $280. The musicians have adopted a saying: "It doesn't matter if it goes platinum or plywood, that's what you get."

There's no royalty for musicians, as you know. And you remember that the Special Payment Fund through the AFM is not based on record sales. It's a formula. Any product that sells over something like a hundred thousand units has to start paying into the fund. It's a tiny, miniscule piece of a penny that goes into the fund for every unit sold above that. The fund is then divided by the total number of master sessions played. The first year, say you do a record, and you do ten sessions to record it. You have ten credits. You take the number of session credits of every musician on the planet that does a session. Then divide the amount of money that was collected by the number of total sessions. It usually comes out to around twenty dollars a session or something like that. That becomes your Special Payments check. It runs for five years. The second year, each session is worth a half a credit. The next year each session would be a quarter of a credit. It disappears after five years. There is still a Special Payments Fund. It doesn't pay out nearly as much as it did twenty years ago for most of us.

What advice do you have for somebody that would want to enter the industry now?

Don't only get as good as you can get on your instrument, but play with other musicians, because your future in music is going to be based on who you're playing with. Be as good and versatile as possible to be prepared to walk through any door that opens, play with as many people as you can.

When you are good enough to be doing those things, record as much as you can in the highest-quality environment that you can afford. If you can afford to get in a real studio, that's great. If not, record in somebody's basement. Every time you record, you will get better at it.

Try to be as creative about making your own audience and place in the music world. Getting on a record label is harder than ever. There are a lot fewer records being cut by labels because of the way the industry has contracted and the difficulty they have in making money on products. You might have to find your own way to make the music available online. Get to the point where people want to buy it—and not just online. Try to make a physical product, if possible. Find places to play that will appeal to your audience. There aren't all the club gigs that used to exist either, unless you want to play country cover music on Lower Broadway in Nashville. There are *a lot* of guys doing that, but, if you have original songs, you are going to have to find your own venues and be creative about marketing yourself.

All those things. And be equally as savvy and versatile in the music business side. If you're interested in being a studio musician or have an artist gig, there are some friends of mine that have done some writing on this subject. Zoro has a book, and now Rich Redmond has a thing out about the music business. I believe he had an article in *Modern Drummer* that is the beginning of his thing. He talks about commitment. Rich is a really good example of knowing how to market himself. He's taken a situation where he's played with an artist and played on some hit records. He's taking those situations and turning that into a clinic career. He's also turned playing on those records into producing other people, like Thompson Square. He's involved in these things. He uses social media, has multiple websites, and understands how the magazines can help him. Anybody starting out now should be prepared to do all of that. Those are things that I didn't have to do when I was getting started.

Any words you would like to share?

I didn't tell any bad stories about anybody . . .

We have time.

[laughs] Next time.

Well, if you get anything out of what I've done, it's that if I can do it, anybody can. If you love it, have a little bit of talent, and work hard at it, then a lot of great things can happen. That's what I did. Here we are almost forty-five years after I started. I still get to do it. Tomorrow morning, I'll get up, set up at Jay's Place, and I'll record. There are a lot worse things you can do on a morning than that.

That's the thing. It's going to be harder than ever to break into session work now. I don't see guys breaking in. The last guy that really did was Rich [Redmond]. Before him, it was Shannon Forrest. Most of the guys that are doing sessions are older guys. That's another way the business has changed. The older guys are hanging on longer than the group before us did. You have to find a different way to break in: with a band or an artist.

Find a way to put the music out there. Use YouTube. You've probably seen Dirty Loops. They are an Internet sensation that got attention by doing cover tunes. They've put their time and talent into playing, obviously, but they know how to use their resources. They figured that more people would be doing a search for Justin Bieber than the Dirty Loops, so they used an opportunity. That's exactly what I've been talking about. That's the kind of good playing, smarts, and savvy that a new musician needs.

Thank you so much, Tommy.

Oh, absolutely!

CONCLUSION

As stated throughout the book, the career of a modern session drummer looks different than it did when the five men interviewed here began their careers. The need to be a technically proficient performer with great adaptability, retention, quickness, creativity, and people skills is still as relevant today as it was at the advent of the modern recording process. The decline in revenue generated by album sales has caused a reduction in the number of albums that are recorded and released in a year. As a result, a musician is unlikely to earn a stable income solely from recording and needs multiple income streams in order to sustain a professional music career.

The genre of country music has diversified and more blatantly incorporates elements typically reserved for other forms of music. As a result, more and more recording artists are "crossing over" to wider commercial audiences as rock, pop, rap, and hip-hop influences further blur the lines of genre. The art form of drumming in Nashville has changed dramatically in the last fifty years to follow suit. Once maligned, the instrument is now firmly set in the rhythm section. Performers have tremendous freedom to experiment with configurations, sounds, and accessories to obtain the right part for each song.

Another significant change is the near necessity for the working professional musician to operate a home-based recording studio to accommodate falling production budgets. There are negatives and positives to this reality. Some of the negatives are that the recordings created in many home studios will not be able to match the quality possible in traditional recording studios due to the inferior acoustic treatment and less sophisticated equipment. Another is the loss of person-to-person chemistry that is created when a group of world-class musicians performs together.

Conversely, there are some positives to the rise of the home studio. A drummer can earn the same rate while also earning money as the owner/operator of the recording studio. There is a degree of comfort that accompanies working from home that is advantageous. Also, with the portability of music files due to the Internet, and the right amount of effective marketing, the potential client base expands across the globe.

It is also likely that the modern professional drummer will write songs; present music clinics and master classes; contribute to journals, magazines, and books; teach private lessons; and balance all of these around a touring schedule with a well-known artist. We may never again see a music industry that produces the number of albums that could sustain the types of careers that Eddie Bayers Jr., Jerry Kroon, Kenny Malone, Tom Roady, and Tommy Wells enjoyed. However, the next generations of drummers will likely be as celebrated for their abilities to inspire and entertain audiences and listeners alike while successfully navigating the challenges and diverse opportunities presented by the modern music industry.

APPENDIX

Who's Who

Willie Ackerman: One of the earliest drummers to appear on *The Grand Ole Opry*. He also appeared on the television show *Hee Haw*. He performed or recorded with Louie Armstrong, Willie Nelson, Waylon Jennings, Charley Pride, Johnny Cash, Slim Whitman, and others.

Chuck Ainlay: Recording, mixing, and mastering engineer. He has recorded, mixed, or mastered albums for such artists and movies as Dire Straits, Reba McEntire, Waylon Jennings, Lyle Lovett, Hank Williams Jr., Trisha Yearwood, *Twister*, *Boys on the Side*, and others.

The Albert Brothers (Ron and Howard): Record producers. Based out of Miami, they worked with many popular artists, including John Cougar Mellencamp, Derek and the Dominos, Pure Prairie League, and Crosby, Stills & Nash.

Joe Allen: Bass guitarist, composer, and vocalist. His songs and performances appear on records by Waylon Jennings, Barbara Mandrell, Don Williams, Gene Watson, George Strait, Crystal Gayle, Glen Campbell, Joe Nichols, and others.

Sam Bacco: Percussionist and drum builder. He performs with the Nashville Symphony. His recording credits include work with New Grass Revival, Travis Tritt, Dolly Parton, Marty Stuart, Garth Brooks, Trisha Yearwood, Jill Sobule, Neil Diamond, Steven Curtis Chapman, Amy Grant, Martina McBride, and others.

Pat Bergeson: Guitarist, harmonica player, and composer. His recording credits include work with Chet Atkins, Bill Frisell, Jeff Coffin Mu'tet, Kenny Rogers, Lyle Lovett, Jo Dee Messina, Suzy Bogguss, Bill Evans, Trace Adkins, Toby Keith, and others.

Hal Blaine: One of the recording session drummers of the Los Angeles–based recording group nicknamed the Wrecking Crew. He is one of the most recorded drummers in history, having appeared on thousands of recordings for musical artists, television productions, and major motion pictures, including work with the Beach Boys, the Ronettes, and Elvis Presley, to name a few.

Jimmy Bowen: Music executive, record producer, recording artist, and composer. He has held executive and upper administration positions at Capitol Records, MGM, Elektra/Asylum, and MCA Records. As an industry executive, he guided the careers of Garth Brooks, Reba McEntire, and George Strait. His production credits include work with Frank Sinatra, Dean Martin, Sammy Davis Jr., Kenny Rogers, Garth Brooks, Reba McEntire, Glen Campbell, Hank Williams Jr., Merle Haggard, Waylon Jennings, and others.

Steve Brewster: Drummer and percussionist. He has recorded with Michael W. Smith, Point of Grace, Bob Seger & the Silver Bullet Band, Richard Marx, Jewel, the Gaither Vocal Band, Kenny Rogers, the Oak Ridge Boys, Willie Nelson, Ricky Skaggs, Toni Braxton, Billy Ray Cyrus, NewSong, FFH, Faith Hill, Cowboy Troy, Chris Tomlin, and others.

David Briggs: Pianist, keyboardist, arranger, and composer. His recording credits include work with Elvis Presley, Kenny Rogers, Earl Scruggs, the Monkees, Percy Sledge, David Allan Coe, Ronnie Milsap, Dobie Gray, Tom Jones, and others. He owned and operated Quadrophonic Recording Studios.

Mike Brignardello: Bass guitarist. His bass playing appears on albums by Amy Grant, Michael W. Smith, Margaret Becker, Kenny Rogers, Steven Curtis Chapman, Dolly Parton, Travis Tritt, Shania Twain, Billy Ray Cyrus, Tim McGraw, Twila Paris, Marty Stuart, Toby Keith, Gretchen Wilson, Jewel, and others.

Roger Brown: Current (as of this writing) president of Berklee College of Music in Boston and recording session drummer.

Tony Brown: Grammy Award–winning music industry executive, record producer, composer, and pianist. He is the former president of MCA Nashville. He served as producer for Shirley Caesar, Reba McEntire, Brooks & Dunn, LeAnn Rimes, Trisha Yearwood, Travis Tritt, Vince Gill, Billy Joel, Michael McDonald, and others. His piano playing can be heard on records by Elvis Presley, Jimmy Buffett, Rodney Crowell, Ricky Skaggs, Roseanne Cash, and others.

Steve Buckingham: Grammy Award–winning record producer, former vice president of A&R for Columbia Records, former senior vice president of A&R at Vanguard and Sugar Hill Records, guitarist, composer, and arranger. His production and recording credits include work with Merle Haggard, Dionne Warwick, Janie Fricke, Ricky Skaggs, Riders in the Sky, Dolly Parton, the Winans, Vince Gill, Gregg Allman, Kirk Whalum, and others.

Fred Buda: Percussion educator who taught at Berklee College of Music and the New England Conservatory in Boston. His performance and recording credits include work with John Williams, the Boston Pops Orchestra, Keith Lockhart, Arthur Fiedler, and others.

Nick Buda: Drummer and percussionist. He has recorded with Taylor Swift, Point of Grace, Jewel, Lionel Richie, Michael W. Smith, Dolly Parton, and others.

Dennis Burnside: Pianist, keyboardist, and arranger. His recording credits include work with Disney, Riders in the Sky, Ricky Skaggs, the Oak Ridge Boys, the Osmonds, Randy Travis, Crystal Gayle, Tanya Tucker, Ray Stevens, Conway Twitty, Aaron Tippin, Martina McBride, the London Symphony Orchestra, Garth Brooks, and others.

Kenny Buttrey: Drummer and percussionist. He appears on albums by Bob Dylan, Elvis Presley, Bob Seger, Al Kooper, Ronnie Hawkins, Gene Cotton, the Earl Scruggs Revue, Jimmy Buffett, Dan Fogelberg, Roy Orbison, and others.

Rick "Moon" Calhoun: Composer, drummer, percussionist, and vocalist. He has written, recorded, or performed with Phil Driscoll, Rufus & Chaka Khan, the Gap Band, and Ray Parker Jr., among others.

Pete Carr: Muscle Shoals–area composer, guitarist, and multi-instrumentalist (string instruments). He was a member of a group of musicians known as the Muscle Shoals Sound Rhythm Section, which started recording at Fame Studio, owned by Rick Hall. The musicians eventually opened their own recording studio called Muscle Shoals Sound Studio. His recording credits include work with Paul Simon, Bob Seger, Dobie Gray, Art Garfunkel, the Staple Singers, Wilson Pickett, Barbara Streisand, Willie Nelson, and others.

Jerry Carrigan: Drummer and percussionist. His recording credits include work with Dolly Parton, Charley Pride, Ray Stevens, the Monkees, Willie Nelson, Kris Kristofferson, Ronnie Hawkins, Gene Cotton, Guy Clark, and others.

Buzz Cason: Record producer, vocalist, composer, and owner of Creative Workshop recording studio. Songs he wrote have been recorded by the Crickets, Mel Tillis, U2, Kenny Rogers, the Beatles, Jerry Lee Lewis, Gloria Estefan, Jan & Dean, and others.

Harold Lee "Curly" Chalker: Recording artist and pedal steel guitarist. His recording credits include work with Doug Kershaw, Charlie McCoy, Lefty Frizell, Buddy Spicher, Waylon Jennings, and others.

Charles "Charlie" Chalmers: Producer, composer, saxophonist, and vocalist who has performed on Grammy Hall of Fame recordings by Aretha Franklin, Al Green, Wilson Pickett, and Dusty Springfield.

Larry Chaney: Guitarist, composer, and producer. His recording and songwriting credits include work with Edwin McCain, Twila Paris & Friends, Gary Puckett, Tracy Nelson, Jay Patten, Rory Block, and others.

Martin Clayton: Current (as of this writing) vice president of Operations and Administration at Country Music Television (CMT) and general manager of CMT.com.

"Cowboy" Jack Clement: Founder of Hall-Clement Music, record producer for Sun Records, composer, and guitarist. He attained legendary status for his production and songwriting work with Johnny Cash, Jerry Lee Lewis, U2, Roy Orbison, George Jones, Carl Perkins, Don Williams, Waylon Jennings, and others.

Billy Cobham: Legendary drummer and composer known for his work with the Mahavishnu Orchestra, John McLaughlin, Jeff Beck, Carlos Santana, Grover Washington Jr., Milt Jackson, George Benson, Miles Davis, and others.

Charles Cochran: Pianist, keyboardist, composer, arranger, and recording artist. His recording credits include work with Garth Brooks, Bobby Goldsboro, Waylon Jennings, Crystal Gayle, Johnny Cash, Kenny Rogers, Don McLean, John Denver, New Grass Revival, Riders in the Sky, and others.

Vinnie Colaiuta: Drummer and percussionist. One of the most influential drummers of the 1970s through the present. He is in the *Modern Drummer* Hall of Fame and has won eighteen Drummer of the Year awards. Notable artists he has worked with include Frank Zappa, Sting, Jeff Beck, Herbie Hancock, Faith Hill, Megadeth, Chick Corea, Joni Mitchell, and others.

Jim Colvard: Electric and acoustic guitarist. His recording credits include work with Doc Watson, Dolly Parton, Charlie McCoy, Kris Kristofferson, Waylon Jennings, Vassar Clements, Gene Cotton, Don Williams, Crystal Gayle, Kenny Rogers, and others.

Stewart Copeland: Drummer, percussionist, record producer, and composer. He is best known for his drumming work with the Police. Other artists whose albums his drumming appears on include Snoop Lion, Roger Daltrey, Peter Gabriel, Tom Waits, Stanley Clarke, and others. He has written music for movie soundtracks, orchestras, and operas.

Sonny Curtis: Composer, guitarist, and vocalist. One of his most notable hits was "I Fought the Law and the Law Won." Songs he wrote were recorded by the Everly Brothers, Fats Waller, the Crickets, Buddy Holly, Glen Campbell, Roy Orbison, Rosanne Cash, Waylon Jennings, the Bobby Fuller Four, Ella Fitgerald, and others.

Danny Dallas: Recording engineer from Detroit. He was the owner of Sound Patterns DXM. His recording credits include work with the Rationals, MC5, Martin Scot Kosins, Jeff Wilkinson, and others.

Wayne Darling: Upright bassist, educator at the University School of Music in Graz, Austria, and recording artist. He has released his own recordings and appeared on albums by Woody Herman, Joe Henderson, Bob Brookmeyer, and others.

Jimmy Darrell: Composer. Songs he wrote appear on records by Alabama, Vern Gosdin, George Strait, the Oak Ridge Boys, and others.

Alan Dawson: Jazz drummer and legendary percussion educator. The "Alan Dawson Method" for the Ted Reed *Syncopation* book is a standard teaching tool for drum set educators. Famed drummers Tony Williams, Vinnie Colaiuta, Steve Smith, Jeff Sipe, and Terri Lynn Carrington are among his former students. He taught at Berklee College of Music in Boston. He performed with Dave Brubeck, Bill Evans, Sonny Rollins, Quincy Jones, and others.

Hank DeVito: Composer, acoustic and electric guitarist, and pedal steel guitarist. He has performed with and written songs for Vince Gill, Juice Newton, Rosanne Cash, Rodney Crowell, Marty Stuart, Don Williams, Ricky Skaggs, Emmylou Harris, and others. He is a member of the Notorious Cherry Bombs and has performed as an instrumentalist on albums by Rosanne Cash and Emmylou Harris.

Jerry Douglas: Record producer, composer, lap steel guitar and dobro player, and vocalist. He is one of Nashville's most in-demand steel guitar and dobro players and can be heard on albums by Garth Brooks, Béla Fleck, Alison Krauss, Randy Travis, Ricky Skaggs, Reba McEntire, and others.

Bob Doyle: Owner and president of Major Bob Music and manager of Garth Brooks. He has held positions at ASCAP and Warner Bros. Records.

Pete Drake: Business executive, record producer, composer, and steel guitarist. He was one of the members of Nashville's "A Team" and the president of Pete Drake Music Group. His production and recording credits include work with Bob Dylan, Ringo Starr, George Harrison, Dolly Parton, Elvis Presley, Bob Wills and the Texas Playboys, Ernest Tubb, David Allan Coe, Jerry Lee Lewis, Lefty Frizell, and others.

Phil Driscoll: Grammy and Dove Award–winning artist, musician (vocals, trumpet), and composer. He has written music with and for Joe Cocker, Blood, Sweat, and Tears, and Billy Preston and led his own band.

Dan Dugmore: Electric and acoustic guitarist, lap and pedal steel guitarist, dobro and banjo player. His recording credits include work with Suzy Bogguss, Linda Rondstadt, James Taylor, the Pointer Sisters, Neil Diamond, Martina McBride, Pam Tillis, Steven Curtis Chapman, Dolly Parton, Kenny Rogers, and others.

Bobby Dyson: Bass guitarist and composer. His recording and song-writing credits include work with Jerry Lee Lewis, Dolly Parton, Kris Kristofferson, Waylon Jennings, Merle Haggard, the Monkees, Lefty Frizell, Porter Wagoner, and others.

Gene Eichelberger: Recording, mixing, and mastering engineer and record producer. His recording credits include work with Bob Seger, Dobie Gray, Kris Kristofferson, Joan Baez, Grand Funk Railroad, Dan Fogelberg, Percy Sledge, Earl Scruggs, Cat Stevens, Jack Clement, Johnny Cash, Amy Grant, Sesame Street, Michael McDonald, Sawyer Brown, Al Green, Disney, Jewel, Lyle Lovett, and others.

Joe English: Drummer, percussionist, and recording artist. His recording credits include work with Paul McCartney, Linda McCartney, Glen Garrett, and his own albums.

Harold Firestone: Drummer, percussionist, and acclaimed percussion educator.

Gary Forkum: Owner of Fork's Drum Closet.

George "Chet" Forrest: Composer and lyricist. He has written for Broadway and musical plays as well as popular music artists. His songs and lyrics can be heard on albums by Ahmad Jamal, Jackie Gleason, the Supremes, the Temptations, Artie Shaw, Glenn Miller, and others.

Shannon Forrest: Drummer, percussionist, and recording engineer. His recording credits include work with Sheryl Crow, Michael McDonald, Gretchen Wilson, Toby Keith, Kenny Rogers, Faith Hill, Brooks & Dunn, Rascal Flatts, Point of Grace, Reba McEntire, Taylor Swift, Carrie Underwood, Blake Shelton, and others. He has toured with Toto, the Dukes of September, Faith Hill, and others.

Fred Foster: Former president of Monument Records, record producer, and composer. His songwriting and production can be heard on records by Willie Nelson, Roy Orbison, Jerry Lee Lewis, Dolly Parton, Kenny Rogers, Ray Stevens, Boots Randolph, Kris Kristofferson, Bill

Anderson, Janis Joplin, Olivia Newton-John, Merle Haggard & the Strangers, and others. He was inducted into the Musicians Hall of Fame and Museum.

Noel Fox: Music industry executive, vocalist, and member of the Oak Ridge Boys. He managed Silverline/Goldine Publishing, was vice president of MCA Music/Nashville, and was president of Maypop Music Group.

Paul Franklin: Lap and pedal steel guitarist and dobro player. His recording credits include work with Dire Straits, Dolly Parton, Riders in the Sky, Marty Stuart, Trisha Yearwood, Martina McBride, Sting, Elton John, Alan Jackson, Faith Hill, Travis Tritt, Ricky Skaggs, and others.

Garth Fundis: Record producer, recording engineer, and former Director of Operations for Almo Sounds Nashville. He has produced and engineered records for artists such as Crystal Gayle, Don Williams, Jack Clement, Emmylou Harris, New Grass Revival, Trisha Yearwood, Alabama, Vince Gill, and others.

Steve Gadd: Drummer, percussionist, composer, and record producer. He is considered one of the most influential drummers of all time for his work with Paul Simon, Steely Dan, George Benson, Chuck Mangione, Aretha Franklin, Paul McCartney, and others. He formed and led several of his own bands over the years, including Stuff and the Gadd Gang.

Ralph Gallant, aka Larrie Londin: Drummer and percussionist. He was perhaps the most important Nashville drummer of the 1970s and 1980s. His recording credits include Chet Atkins, Waylon Jennings, B.B. King, Vince Gill, Roseanne Cash, Reba McEntire, Steve Perry, Willie Nelson, and others.

Robert John Gallo: Record producer, recording artist, and composer. His production credits include work with Dust and his own albums.

Albhy Galuten: Grammy Award–winning record producer, composer, and arranger. He has produced, recorded, and performed with Aretha Franklin, Olivia Newton-John, the Eagles, Barbara Streisand, Eric Clapton, Dolly Parton, No Doubt, and others.

Sonny Garrish: Steel guitarist, dobro player, and pedal steel guitarist. His recording credits include work with Toby Keith, Tim McGraw, George Strait, Bryan White, Kenny Rogers, Billy Ray Cyrus, Tanya Tucker, Janie Fricke, Lee Roy Parnell, George Jones, Don Williams, Sawyer Brown, the Judds, B.B. King, Ray Stevens, and others.

Steve Gibson: Guitarist. His recording credits include work with Ray Price, Dolly Parton, Willie Nelson, George Strait, Tanya Tucker, Kenny Rogers, Martina McBride, Ray Stevens, Roy Orbison, Shelby Lynne, Disney, Glen Campbell, Reba McEntire, Vince Gill, and others. He also leads his own band, called Steve Gibson & the Red Caps.

Jim Gordon: Drummer, percussionist, and composer. Toured or recorded with Frank Zappa, Delaney & Bonnie, Joe Cocker, Derek & the Dominos, Neil Diamond, the Monkees, the Muppets, Alice Cooper, Daryl Hall & John Oates, Carole King, John Lennon, B.B. King, and others. He wrote and played the piano coda on the Derek & the Dominos song "Layla." He was an undiagnosed paranoid schizophrenic whose career was cut short after he murdered his mother in the early 1980s. He remains incarcerated as of this writing.

Freddie Gruber: Percussion educator who pioneered an ergonomic approach to percussion performance. Neil Peart, Dave Weckl, Vinnie Colaiuta, and Steve Smith are among his former students.

John Guerin: Drummer and percussionist. His recording credits include work with the Brady Bunch, Gerry Mulligan, the Monkees, Frank Zappa, Harry Nilsson, Joni Mitchell, Larry Carlton, Art Garfunkel, the Oak Ridge Boys, Milt Jackson, the Everly Brothers, and others.

Jeff Hamilton: Recording artist, drummer, percussionist, and composer. Leader of the Jeff Hamilton Trio, his recording credits include work with Diana Krall, Paul McCartney, Norah Jones, Willie Nelson, Johnny Mercer, Natalie Cole, Nina Simone, Monty Alexander, Michael Bublé, Queen Latifah, Gladys Knight, Mel Tormé, Joey DeFrancesco, and others.

Glen D. Hardin: Pianist, keyboardist, arranger, and composer. His recording credits include work with Elvis Presley, Johnny Cash, Marty Stuart, Dwight Yoakam, John Denver, Emmylou Harris, Buddy Holly & the Crickets, Dean Martin, and others.

Buddy Harman: He is possibly the most recorded drummer in history, having been hired for over eighteen thousand sessions. He pioneered drums on country music recordings and is credited as the inventor of the drumming "Country Shuffle." Some of the notable artists he worked with include Elvis Presley, Roy Orbison, Patsy Cline, the Everly Brothers, and Johnny Cash.

Bud Harner: Drummer, percussionist, composer, and record producer. His work can be heard on records by Barry Manilow, Spyro Gyra, David Benoit, Keiko Matsui, George Benson, Jeff Lorber, and others.

Roger Hawkins: Muscle Shoals–area drummer, composer, recording studio owner, and record producer. He was a member of a group of musicians known as the Muscle Shoals Sound Rhythm Section, which started recording at Fame Studio, owned by Rick Hall. The musicians eventually opened their own recording studio called Muscle Shoals Sound Studio. Hawkins has recorded or produced albums by Aretha Franklin, the Rolling Stones, Ray Charles, Bob Seger, Paul Simon, Eric Clapton, Wilson Pickett, the Staple Singers, and others.

Lee Hazen: Owner of recording studio Studio by the Pond, recording engineer, and record producer. His recording credits include Bobby Goldsboro, Doc Watson, Dan Fogelberg, Jimmy Buffett, Linda Rondstadt, George Jones, Tracy Nelson, and others.

Neil Hefti: Jazz musician (trumpet), composer, and arranger known for his work with popular jazz big bands like Count Basie and Woody Herman, and for scoring for film and television. Some of his major credits include music for the *Batman* television series and the *Odd Couple* movie and television series.

Karl Himmel: Drummer and percussionist. His recording credits include work with Bob Dylan, Jimmy Buffett, the Charlie Daniels Band, Earl Scruggs, the Doobie Brothers, Neil Young, Ricky Skaggs, George Jones, J.J. Cale, Lefty Frizell, Harry Nilsson, and others.

John Hobbs: Pianist, keyboardist, arranger, and record producer. He is a ten-time Keyboard Player of the Year, awarded by the Academy of Country Music. His recording credits include work with Michael Bolton, Vince Gill, Amy Grant, Alison Krauss, Point of Grace, Joan Osborne, Peter Cetera, B.B. King, Lynyrd Skynyrd, Keith Urban, Kenny Rogers, Shania Twain, Cher, and others.

Major Holley: Bass guitarist and educator at Berklee College of Music in Boston. His recording credits include work with Clark Terry, Coleman Hawkins, Kenny Burrell, Quincy Jones, Duke Ellington, Roy Eldridge, Bob James, Doctor Billy Dodd, Stanley Turrentine, Zoot Sims, Jo Jones, and others.

David Hood: Muscle Shoals–area bass guitarist. He was a member of a group of musicians known as the Muscle Shoals Sound Rhythm Section, which started recording at Fame Studio, owned by Rick Hall. The musicians eventually opened their own recording studio called Muscle Shoals Sound Studio. Hood has recorded or produced albums by Aretha Franklin, the Rolling Stones, Ray Charles, Bob Seger, Paul Simon, Eric Clapton, Wilson Pickett, the Staple Singers, and others.

James Hooker: Pianist, composer, and singer. He was a member of the Amazing Rhythm Aces and has composed or recorded music with Nanci Griffith, Steve Winwood, John Hiatt, Emmylou Harris, Sawyer Brown, and others.

Trevor Horn: Record producer, band member in Yes and the Buggles, vocalist, and composer. His production, songwriting, and recording credits include work with Yes, the Buggles, Grace Jones, Rod Stewart, Simple Minds, Paul McCartney, Hans Zimmer, the London Philharmonic Orchestra, Seal, Barry Manilow, Tina Turner, and others. He is a cofounder of ZZT Records.

Harlan Howard: Composer. He is possibly the most successful songwriter in country music history. Among the many hit songs he wrote are "I Fall to Pieces," "Busted," "I've Got a Tiger by the Tail," and "Heartaches by the Number." He is a member of the Nashville Songwriters Hall of Fame and the Country Music Hall of Fame.

Dann Huff: Vocalist, guitarist, record producer, arranger, and recording engineer. He was a founding member of the band Whiteheart. His recording and production credits include work with Kenny Rogers, Amy Grant, Barbara Streisand, Phil Driscoll, Michael W. Smith, Whitney Houston, Faith Hill, Madonna, the Temptations, Peter Cetera, Tiffany, Michael Jackson, Chicago, Vanessa Williams, Boyz II Men, Megadeth, Celine Dion, Keith Urban, and others.

Bill Humble: Bass guitarist. His recording credits include work with J.J. Cale, Vassar Clements, Sleepy LaBeef, Hank Mizell, and others.

Ralph Humphrey: Drummer and percussionist. He can be heard on recordings by Frank Zappa, Gap Mangione, Pages, Al Jarreau, José Feliciano, Wayne Shorter, the Muppets, and John Denver. His television credits include work on *Dancing with the Stars* and *American Idol.*

Mitch Humphries: Composer, pianist, and keyboardist. He has appeared on recordings with Charley Pride, Dolly Parton, George Strait, Vern Gosdin, Reba McEntire, Lorrie Morgan, Tanya Tucker, the Gaither Vocal Band, Aaron Tippin, Ronnie Milsap, and others.

Dave Hungate: Bass guitarist and composer. He was a founding member of the band Toto. His bass playing can be heard on records by Sonny & Cher, Boz Scaggs, the Righteous Brothers, Rickie Lee Jones, Barry Manilow, Billy Preston, Joe Cocker, and others.

John Jarvis: Pianist, keyboardist, and composer. He can be heard on recordings by Vince Gill, Art Garfunkel, Kenny Rogers, Jimmy Buffett, Hank Williams Jr., George Strait, Reba McEntire, the Judds, Mark O'Connor, John Denver, and others.

Darryl Johnson: Vocalist, composer, recording engineer, and multi-instrumentalist. His recording credits include work with Bob Dylan, Aaron Neville, Emmylou Harris, Brian Blade, Linda Rondstadt, Brian Eno, Boz Scaggs, and others.

Doug Johnson: Current (as of this writing) head of A&R at Curb Records, record producer, recording engineer, and composer. His album credits include work with Dolly Parton, Ricky Skaggs, Tim McGraw, Ty Herndon, Sons of the Desert, Hank Williams Jr., Randy Travis, and others.

William Everett "Bill" Justis: Former A&R representative for Sun Records and Mercury record labels, record producer, and composer. His production, songwriting, and arrangements can be heard on albums by Johnny Cash, Boots Randolph, George Harrison, Dean Martin, Conway Twitty, Jerry Lee Lewis, Kenny Rogers & the First Edition, Don McLean, John Denver, and others. His song "Raunchy" is in the Grammy Hall of Fame.

Shane Keister: Pianist, keyboardist, record producer, arranger, and engineer. His recording and production credits include work with Alan Jackson, Crystal Gayle, Kenny Rogers, Johnny Cash, Amy Grant, Jimmy Buffett, Earl Scruggs, Olivia Newton-John, Gene Cotton, Steve Wariner, Rosanne Cash, Tom Jones, Sawyer Brown, Randy Travis, Delbert McClinton, and others. He is a member of the Musicians Hall of Fame and Museum.

Jim Keltner: Drummer, percussionist, and composer. He has toured or recorded with John Lennon, Ry Cooder, Celine Dion, Mavis Staples, Joe Cocker, Jerry Lee Lewis, Roy Orbison, Willie Nelson, Bob Dylan, Rickie Lee Jones, Fiona Apple, Steely Dan, Randy Newman, Simon & Garfunkel, B.B. King, Eric Clapton, Bill Frisell, and others.

Bobby Keys: Saxophonist. He is well known for his work with the Rolling Stones. His recording credits include work with Eric Clapton, the Rolling Stones, Harry Nilsson, Delaney & Bonnie, B.B. King, Yoko Ono, John Lennon, Ringo Starr, Marvin Gaye, Joe Cocker, Maroon 5, Keith Richards, and others.

Al Kiger: Composer and trumpet and flugelhorn player. His recording credits include work with Ornette Coleman, George Russell, Liz Antony, Royce Campbell, John Lewis, and others.

Buddy Killen: Former owner of Trinity Broadcast Network, Killen Music Group, and Tree Publishing, composer, and record producer. His producing and songwriting credits include albums for Johnny Cash, Conway Twitty, Faron Young, Jerry Lee Lewis, Elvis Presley, George Jones, Joe Tex, Bill Anderson, Kenny Rogers, Ray Price, T.G. Sheppard, Patsy Cline, and others.

Brent King: Recording and mixing engineer. His recording credits include work with Ricky Skaggs, Steve Green, FFH, Earl Scruggs, Martina McBride, Keith Urban, Kirk Franklin, Lakewood Church, Michael W. Smith, Glen Campbell, the Brooklyn Tabernacle Choir, Bobby Jones & the New Life Singers, Reba McEntire, and others.

Ed Kotowski: Drummer with Phil Driscoll and many other bands in the St. Louis area, namely, Spirit of St. Louis and Z.

Gene Krupa: Popular drummer from the big band era of jazz. He is perhaps best known for his performance of "Sing, Sing, Sing" with Benny Goodman and was a charismatic leader of his own big band.

Gary Langan: Record producer, composer, and recording and mixing engineer. His production, songwriting, and recording credits include work with Gene Simmons, Snoop Dogg, Billy Idol, Yes, Natalie Imbruglia, and others. He is a cofounder of ZZT Records.

Nelson Larkin: Record producer and composer. His production and songwriting credits include work with Earl Thomas Conley, Billy Joe Royal, George Jones, Tracy Lawrence, Toby Keith, Alabama, and others.

Mike Lawler: Pianist, keyboardist, and composer. He has recorded or composed music with the Allman Brothers Band, Kenny Rogers, the Pointer Sisters, Steve Winwood, Alabama, Hank Williams Jr., Delbert McClinton, Michael W. Smith, Sawyer Brown, Chet Atkins, Garth Brooks, Shawn Mullins, and others.

Gene Lawson: Composer, drummer, recording engineer. Primarily a songwriter, songs he wrote have been recorded by Otis Redding and others. He is the former owner of Reflections Recording Studio, located in the Berry Hill area of Nashville.

Mike Leech: Bass guitarist and arranger. He rose to prominence recording in Memphis. His recording credits include work with Dionne Warwick, Elvis Presley, Dobie Gray, Ray Stevens, Willie Nelson, George Strait, Tom Jones, Roy Orbison, and others.

Paul Leim: Drummer and percussionist. His drumming can be heard on records by the Beach Boys, Amy Grant, Lionel Richie, Peter Cetera, Kenny Rogers, Michael W. Smith, Diana Ross, Whitney Houston, Michael Card, Rich Mullins, Steven Curtis Chapman, Shania Twain, Reba McEntire, Point of Grace, and others.

Larrie Londin: See *Ralph Gallant, aka Larrie Londin.*

Steve Lukather: Composer, vocalist, guitarist, record producer, and member of Grammy Award–winning band Toto. He has recorded with Michael Jackson, Paul McCartney, Lionel Richie, Boz Scaggs, Steely Dan, Rickie Lee Jones, Don Henley, Elton John, Eric Clapton, and others.

Ralph MacDonald: Percussionist, composer, and record producer. He performed on recordings by Aretha Franklin, Art Garfunkel, Billy Joel, Quincy Jones, Lionel Richie, Jimmy Buffett, and others. Songs he composed appear on albums by Amy Winehouse, Grover Washington Jr., Lou Rawls, and others.

Brent Maher: Record producer, recording engineer, composer, and arranger. His production and recording credits include work with Kenny Rogers, Juice Newton, Wes Montgomery, Ray Charles, Bobby Darin, Ike & Tina Turner, Olivia Newton-John, Gene Cotton, the Judds, and others.

Grady Martin: Electric and acoustic guitarist, composer, and record producer. He is one of the most recorded guitarists in history as a member of Nashville's "A Team." His recording credits include work with Brenda Lee, Roy Orbison, Ernest Tubb & the Texas Troubadors, Patsy Cline, Ray Price, Elvis Presley, Porter Wagoner, Henry Mancini, Arlo Guthrie, Loretta Lynn, and others.

Billy Mason: Drummer and percussionist. He is a member of Tim McGraw's touring band. Past tours include Faith Hill, Bill Anderson, and others.

Brent Mason: Guitarist, recording artist, and composer. He has played guitar on numerous television commercials, and his film credits include *A Few Good Men*, *Ferris Bueller's Day Off*, *The Prince of Egypt*, *Son in Law*, *Home Alone*, and others. His work with major artists includes John Fogerty, Kenny Rogers, Alan Jackson, Martina McBride, John Rich, Blake Shelton, the Gaither Vocal Band, Amy Grant, Lee Ann Womack, Rascal Flatts, the Players, Lane Brody, Alabama, Faith Hill, and others.

George Massenburg: Record producer; recording, mixing, and mastering engineer; and owner of George Massenburg Labs (GML). He has produced or engineered albums by Philip Glass, Stanley Clarke, Aaron Neville, Ry Cooder, Little Feat, Ricky Skaggs, Cher, James Taylor, Journey, Earth, Wind & Fire, Carly Simon, and others.

Bob Mater: Drummer, percussionist, record producer, and composer. He has toured or recorded with Paul Reed Smith, Sam Levine, New Grass Revival, Dolly Parton, Riders in the Sky, Boots Randolph, Chet

Atkins, Mark O'Connor, Pat Coil, the Jordanaires, Disney, Béla Fleck, Kathy Trocolli, and others.

Greg Mathieson: Arranger, record producer, composer, and keyboardist/pianist. He has composed for or recorded with artists such as Al Jarreau, Les Paul, Donna Summer, Engelbert Humperdinck, Quincy Jones, Phil Driscoll, Cher, Tower of Power, Ringo Starr, Tina Turner, the Commodores, Diana Ross, and others.

Danny Matousek: Composer and guitarist. Founding member of the Velaires, which became known as the Flairs, of "Roll Over Beethoven" fame.

John McBride: Owner of Blackbird Studio, recording and mixing engineer, and production coordinator. Blackbird Studio is one of the finest recording facilities in Nashville. Artists who have recorded there include Justin Bieber, Kesha, R.E.M., Bruce Springsteen, Martina McBride, and Keith Urban.

Charlie McCoy: Harmonica, composer, and multi-instrumentalist. His recording credits include work with Bob Dylan, Roy Orbison, Waylon Jennings, Joan Osborne, Paul Simon, Jerry Lee Lewis, Johnny Cash, Randy Travis, Dan Fogelberg, Ween, Brenda Lee, Patsy Cline, Reba McEntire, Gene Cotton, the Statler Brothers, Ringo Starr, Quincy Jones, and others. He was a founding member of Area Code 615 and Barefoot Jerry.

Kevin McManus: President of Nashville Teleproductions Inc. and Zion Music Group, recording and mixing engineer, and composer. His recording credits include work with the Marshall Tucker Band, Charlie McCoy, Gene Watson, Bill & Gloria Gaither, Willie Nelson, Ray Price, and others.

Mitch Mitchell: Drummer who is best known for his work with the Jimi Hendrix Experience.

Bob Montgomery: Founder of House of Gold Publishing, record producer, guitarist, and recording engineer. His credits as a songwriter, producer, or guitarist include work with Buddy Holly, Patsy Cline, Cliff Richard, Loretta Lynn, Shelby Lynne, Bobby Goldsboro, Suzy Bogguss, Merle Haggard, Boyz II Men, and others. His publishing company published such hits as "Wind Beneath My Wings," "Love in the First Degree," and others.

Bob Moore: Bass guitarist, record producer, orchestra leader, and composer. He is one of the most recorded bass players in history as a member of Nashville's "A Team." He has contributed to recordings by Chet Atkins, Roy Orbison, Elvis Presley, Brenda Lee, Patsy Cline, Roger Miller, Bob Wills & His Texas Playboys, Bob Dylan, and others.

Dale Morris: Artist manager, owner of WeBlast Records, and owner of the Tracking Room recording studio. He has managed Kenny Chesney, Alabama, Gretchen Wilson, and Big & Rich.

Farrell Morris: Percussionist. His recording credits include work with Ray Stevens, Elvis Presley, Kris Kristofferson, Dan Fogelberg, Joan Baez, Jimmy Buffett, Sandi Patty, Chet Atkins, Dolly Parton, Ronnie Milsap, Gene Cotton, Willie Nelson, the Oak Ridge Boys, Neil Young, Amy Grant, Tom Jones, Hank Williams Jr., and others.

Mark Morris: Percussionist and composer. His recording credits include work with Suzy Bogguss, Johnny Cash, George Jones, the Allman Brothers Band, Dolly Parton, and others.

Wayne Moss: Guitarist, composer, record producer, and engineer. His recording and production credits include work with Peter, Paul and Mary, Patsy Cline, Chet Atkins, Porter Wagoner, Dolly Parton, Charley Pride, Roy Orbison, the Monkees, Little Jimmy Dickens, Willie Nelson, and others. Songs he has written appear on records by Charlie McCoy, Barefoot Jerry, Tommy Emmanuel, Chet Atkins, and others. He was a founding member of Area Code 615 and Barefoot Jerry.

Edgar Myer: Grammy Award–winning bassist, arranger, composer, and recording artist. Myer's work can be heard with Béla Fleck, James Taylor, Yo-Yo Ma, Wynton Marsalis, Nickel Creek, Travis Tritt, New Grass Revival, Garth Brooks, as well as on his own records.

Jamie Nichol: Percussionist. His recording credits include work with Charlie Daniels, Moe Denham, Dolly Parton, the Marshall Tucker Band, and others.

Jim Ed Norman: Former president of Warner Bros. Nashville and Leadership Music, record producer, composer, and educator. His production credits include albums by the Eagles, Janie Fricke, Linda

Rondstadt, the Osmonds, Hank Williams Jr., Crystal Gayle, Glenn Frey, Garth Brooks, Kenny Rogers, and others.

Ron Oates: Pianist, keyboardist, arranger, and composer. His recording credits include work with Dolly Parton, Ray Stevens, Gene Cotton, the Oark Ridge Boys, Earl Thomas Conley, Glady Knight & the Pips, and others.

Bobby Ogden: Pianist and keyboardist. His recording credits include work with Kenny Rogers, the Perrys, Gene Cotton, the Jordanaires, and others.

Jamie Oldaker: Drummer, percussionist, record producer. He is well known for his work with Bob Seger and Eric Clapton. He played on such hits as "Wonderful Tonight," "I Shot the Sheriff," and "Cocaine." He is also credited with working with New Grass Revival, Ace Frehley, Leon Russel, and Peter Frampton.

Nigel Olsson: Drummer and percussionist. He is best known for his long association with Elton John. He has recorded with Elton John, Rod Stewart, Linda Rondstadt, Neil Sedaka, and others. He has also released six of his own albums.

Paul Overstreet: Composer. Songs that he wrote appear on albums by Kenny Chesney, George Jones, Blake Shelton, Tanya Tucker, Alison Krauss & Union Station, Randy Travis, Lee Greenwood, and others. Notable hits include "When You Say Nothing at All" and "Same Ole Me."

Sergio Pastora: Percussionist. He recorded or toured with such artists as Eric Clapton, Bob Seger, Gino Vanelli, the Section, and Phil Driscoll.

Larry Paxton: Bass guitarist, composer, and arranger. His recording credits include work with Ricky Van Shelton, Kenny Rogers, Disney, Kenny Chesney, Alabama, Bob Seger, David Allan Coe, George Strait, Alabama, Ricky Skaggs, Bill Anderson, George Jones, and others.

Stu Perry: Drummer. He has recorded with Delaney Bramlett, Dwight Yoakam, Johnny Turner, and others.

Jim Pettit: Owner of Memphis Drum Shop (as of this writing).

Dave Pomeroy: President of the American Federation of Musicians #257 (as of this writing), bass guitarist, and vocalist. He has performed on records by Jim Horn, Don Williams, Lorrie Morgan, Alan Jackson, Emmylou Harris, Alison Krauss, Trisha Yearwood, Don McLean, Kenny Rogers, Billy Ray Cyrus, Randy Scruggs, Dobie Gray, and others.

Robert "Pops" Popwell: Composer and bass guitarist who was a member of the Young Rascals and the Crusaders. He also recorded with George Benson, B.B. King, Bette Midler, Larry Carlton, Aretha Franklin, and others.

Jeff Porcaro: Recording session drummer and member of Grammy Award–winning band Toto. He has recorded with Michael Jackson, Madonna, Boz Scaggs, Steely Dan, Rickie Lee Jones, Don Henley, Bruce Springsteen, Elton John, Eric Clapton, and others.

Joe Porcaro: Percussion. His work can be heard on recordings by the Monkees, Don Ellis, Bonnie Raitt, Boz Scaggs, Olivia Newton-John, Toto, Stan Getz, Freddie Hubbard, Crystal Gayle, James Newton Howard, Harry Connick Jr., Bette Midler, Richard Marx, and others. He is cochair of the Drum Department at the Los Angeles College of Music.

Richard Dean "Rick" Powell: Guitarist, synthesizer, record producer, and arranger. His recording and production credits include work with the Oak Ridge Boys, the Bill Gaither Trio, Pat Boone, and others.

Gary Prim: Pianist, keboardist, and composer. His recording credits include work with Ray Stevens, Vern Gosdin, Reba McEntire, Jack Greene, Tim McGraw, Kenny Rogers, Willie Nelson, NewSong, Billy Ray Cyrus, Alan Jackson, the Gaither Vocal Band, Lorrie Morgan, George Jones, and others.

Brian Pruitt: Drummer and percussionist. His recording credits include work with Pam Tillis, Lee Brice, Melanie Denard, Randy Kohrs, Josh Gracin, Beth Neilsen Chapman, LeAnn Rimes, Aaron Neville, Luke Bryan, and others.

Bernard "Pretty" Purdie: Drummer, percussionist, and recording artist. He is a highly regarded drummer who has recorded with James Brown, Aretha Franklin, Steely Dan, Nina Simone, Jimmy Smith, Quincy Jones, Grover Washington Jr., Cat Stevens, Miles Davis, Joe Cocker, the Bee Gees, B.B. King, and others.

Claude "Curly" Putman: Composer. Songs that he wrote appear on albums by Charley Pride, Dolly Parton, Randy Travis, George Jones, Jerry Lee Lewis, Tom Jones, Kenny Rogers, T. Graham Brown, Porter Wagoner, and others.

Ricky Ray Rector: Composer and guitarist. He has recorded or composed music with Etta James, the Band, George Strait, Dobie Gray, T. Graham Brown, and others.

Rich Redmond: Drummer and percussionist. He tours and records with Jason Aldean. His recording credits include work with Alabama, Thompson Square, Trace Adkins, Montgomery Gentry, Doc Walker, and others.

Allen Reynolds: Record producer, composer, and vocalist. His production and songwriting credits include work with Garth Brooks, Jerry Garcia, B.B. King, Jerry Lee Lewis, Waylon Jennings, Don Williams, Lefty Frizell, Loretta Lynn, Crystal Gayle, and others. He is an inductee into the Nashville Songwriters Hall of Fame.

Ron "Snake" Reynolds: Record producer and recording engineer. His recording and production credits include work with Elvis Costello, Merle Haggard, George Jones, Johnny Cash, and others.

Danny Rhodes: Guitarist and composer. He is the founder of Nashville-based band the Nerve. He released several of his own albums as well as contributed to projects with Etta James and others.

Michael Rhodes: Bass guitarist. He has recorded with Dolly Parton, Hank Williams Jr., Reba McEntire, Alabama, Kenny Rogers, Richard Marx, Jill Sobule, Delbert McClinton, Vince Gill, Larry Carlton, Faith Hill, Peter Cetera, Shawn Colvin, and others.

Buddy Rich: Regarded by many as the greatest drummer to ever live. He was a child prodigy, and his career began at a young age billed as "Traps the Drum Wonder" when he was just eighteen months old. He led his own jazz big band for many years. He also toured or recorded with Tommy Dorsey, Artie Shaw, Ella Fitzgerald, Nat King Cole, Art Tatum, Lionel Hampton, Oscar Peterson, Charlie Parker, Sammy Davis Jr., Stan Kenton, Count Basie, Mel Tormé, and others over the course of his sixty-plus-year career.

Karl Richardson: Grammy Award–winning record producer and recording engineer. He was voted Producer of the Year in 1978. *Saturday Night Fever*, on which Richardson was producer and engineer, won Album of the Year. He has recorded and produced such artists as the Bee Gees, Kenny Rogers, Dionne Warwick, Barbara Streisand, Frankie Valli, and others.

Hargus "Pig" Robbins: One of the most recorded pianists/keyboardists of all time. He was a member of Nashville's "A Team" of recording session musicians. His recording credits include work with Dolly Parton, Ernest Tubb & the Texas Troubadors, Charley Pride, Willie Nelson, the Statler Brothers, the Everly Brothers, Leon Russell, Loretta Lynn, Ronnie Milsap, and others.

Joe Romano: Composer, multi-instrumentalist (woodwinds, brass, bass guitar, and guitar), arranger, and record producer. His recording credits include work with Louis Bellson, Buddy Rich, Woody Herman, Tom Waits, Chuck Mangione, James Brown, Tito Puente, Dizzy Gillespie, and others.

Dan Rudin: Producer, recording engineer, and mixing engineer. He is the owner of Dan Rudin Recording & Production. He has recorded or produced music for projects by Donnie McClurkin, Veggie Tales, Newsboys, Disney, Riders in the Sky, the Players, High School Musical, Natalie Grant, and others.

Chuck Sabatino: St. Louis–area musician, vocalist, and composer. He collaborated with Michael McDonald, John Tesh, Vince Gill, David Benoit, and others.

Merl Saunders: Pianist, keyboardist, record producer, recording artist, and owner of Sumertone Records. He has written songs for, recorded, and toured with the Grateful Dead, Jerry Garcia, Frank Sinatra, Miles Davis, Taj Mahal, Tom Fogerty, and Betty Davis as well as released his own records.

Mark Schatz: Bass guitarist, record producer, composer, and arranger. His recording credits include work with Béla Fleck, Doc Watson, Nickel Creek, Jerry Douglas, Mark O'Connor, Alison Brown, and others.

Randy Scruggs: Acoustic and electric guitarist, record producer, composer, and recording engineer. His production, songwriting, and recording credits include work with Johnny Cash, Earl Scruggs (his father), Waylon Jennings, Hank Williams Jr., Earl Thomas Conley, Rosanne Cash, Sawyer Brown, Emmylou Harris, George Strait, Vince Gill, Kellie Pickler, Toby Keith, Sara Evans, the Dixie Chicks, and others.

Kirby Shelstad: Composer, engineer, and percussionist. He has recorded Béla Fleck, Leon Russel, John Jarvis, Jill Sobule, Beth Nielsen Chapman, and others.

Billy Sherrill: Record producer, composer, and arranger. His production, songwriting, and arranging credits can be heard on albums by Johnny Cash, Ronnie Milsap, Waylon Jennings, Merle Haggard, George Jones, Tammy Wynette, John Denver, Martina McBride, and others. He is an inductee into the Musicians Hall of Fame and Museum.

Billy Sherrill: Recording engineer. His recording credits include work with Kenny Rogers, Jason Crabb, Roy Clark, Waylon Jennings, Kenny Chesney, Donna Fargo, and others.

Dick Sims: Organist and keyboardist. He is well known for his work with Bob Seger and Eric Clapton. He played on such hits as "Wonderful Tonight," "I Shot the Sheriff," and "Cocaine." He is also credited with working with Freddie King, Sammy Hagar, and Joan Armatrading.

Leland Sklar: Bass guitarist and composer. He has written music that has appeared in *The Prince of Egypt*, *The Postman*, *Legally Blonde*, *For Love of the Game*, and other films. As a bass guitarist, he has performed and recorded with James Taylor, Phil Collins, Lyle Lovett, Don Henley, Faith Hill, Rod Stewart, Vince Gill, Ricky Skaggs, the Doors, Crosby, Stills & Nash, and others.

David Smith: Bass guitarist, composer, record producer, arranger, and vocalist. His recording credits include work with Don McLean, Bill Gaither, Russ Taff, Willie Nelson, Ray Price, Gene Watson, Jonny Lang, the Oak Ridge Boys, and others.

Roddy Smith: Guitarist. He has performed and recorded with Bill Evans, Bonnie Bramlett, Willie Nelson, Boots Randolph, Mr. Groove, the Detroit-Memphis Experience, and others.

Tim Smith: Bass player and record producer. He has performed and recorded with Bill Evans, Bonnie Bramlett, Willie Nelson, Boots Randolph, Mr. Groove, the Detroit-Memphis Experience, and others.

Mike Stewart: Record producer, composer, guitarist, and recording engineer. His production and recording credits include work with Billy Joel, Ronnie Milsap, Rosanne Cash, the Dead Milkmen, Tom Jones, and others.

Richard Tee: Pianist, keyboardist, composer, and arranger. He was a founding member of the band Stuff. He recorded with many artists, including Quincy Jones, Nina Simone, Grover Washington Jr., Aretha Franklin, Joe Cocker, Paul Simon, George Harrison, Blood, Sweat, and Tears, Billy Joel, Gladys Knight & the Pips, Barbara Streisand, Chaka Khan, Spyro Gyra, Peter Gabriel, David Bowie, Michael Bolton, Mariah Carey, and others.

Bobby Thompson: Guitarist and banjo player. His recording credits include albums by the Monkees, the Steve Miller Band, Willie Nelson, Elvis Presley, Dolly Parton, Waylon Jennings, the Pointer Sisters, Chet Atkins, Jimmy Buffett, Gene Cotton, the Oak Ridge Boys, Jerry Lee Lewis, Randy Travis, Merle Haggard, and others.

Richard Tokatz: St. Louis–based percussionist. He has appeared on records by Karizma and David Garfield.

Rafe Van Hoy: Composer. He has written songs that have been recorded by Suzy Bogguss, Tanya Tucker, the Oak Ridge Boys, Sawyer Brown, Glen Campbell, Tracey Ullman, Donna Summer, Fleetwood Mac, George Jones, LeAnn Rimes, and others. "Baby I Lied," "Cryin' Again," "I Hurt for You," and "Let's Stop Talkin' About It" are among the songs that he has written.

Carlos Vega: Drummer and percussionist. Respected among his peers for his outstanding groove, Vega can be heard on records by Cher, James Taylor, Chet Atkins, Reba McEntire, Vince Gill, Bette Midler, Ricky Martin, Lee Ritenour, Diana Ross, Aaron Neville, and others.

Jim Vest: Composer, record producer, guitarist (pedal steel, lap steel), and arranger. His production, songwriting, and recording credits include work with Janie Fricke, George Jones, Kansas, Vern Gosdin, the

Statler Brothers, Tim McGraw, Alan Jackson, Lorrie Morgan, and others.

Bill Vitt: Drummer, producer, arranger, and composer. His credits include work with Merl Saunders, Tom Fogerty, Jerry Garcia, and others.

Biff Watson: Acoustic and electric guitarist and banjo player. His recording credits include work with Reba McEntire, SHeDAISY, Faith Hill, Billy Ray Cyrus, George Strait, Kenny Chesney, Peter Cetera, Alabama, Aaron Tippin, the Gaither Vocal Band, Don McLean, Crystal Gayle, and George Jones.

Jimmy Webb: Grammy Award–winning composer and vocalist. He has written many hit songs, including "MacArthur Park," recorded by Richard Harris (1968) and Donna Summer (1978); "Wichita Lineman," recorded by Glen Campbell; "All I Know," recorded by Art Garfunkel; and many others.

Dave Weckl: Recording artist, drummer, composer, and arranger. He is well known for his work with Chick Corea, Michel Camilo, Mike Stern, John Patitucci, and Frank Gambale as well as on his own albums.

Jerry Wexler: Grammy Award–winning producer, composer, and journalist. He produced or composed music for Aretha Franklin, George Benson, Patti Labelle & the Bluebelles, Ray Charles, Derek & the Dominos, Carole King, Willie Nelson, Bob Dylan, Rod Stewart, and others.

Neil Wilburn: Record producer and recording engineer. His production and recording credits include work with the Byrds, Johnny Cash, Earl Scruggs, Vassar Clements, Waylon Jennings, Shirley Caesar, Pete Seeger, Bob Dylan, and others.

Mentor Williams: Grammy Award–winning record producer and composer. His songwriting and production credits include Dobie Gray, the Ventures, Michael Bolton, the Neville Brothers, Randy Travis, George Jones, Roy Orbison, Ike & Tina Turner, Rod Stewart, and others.

Ernie Winfrey: Recording engineer. His engineering credits include Wilson Pickett, Chet Atkins, Lee Greenwood, Levon Helm, Dolly Parton, Neil Young, and others.

Bobby Woods: Pianist, keyboardist, and composer. He rose to prominence recording in Memphis. His recording credits include work with Bob Seger, Ronnie Milsap, Don McLean, Wilson Pickett, Eric Clapton, and others.

Glenn Worf: Record producer and bass guitarist. His recording credits include work with Faith Hill, Alabama, Kenny Rogers, Alison Krauss, Marty Stuart, Brenda Lee, Martina McBride, Trisha Yearwood, Alan Jackson, Shania Twain, Brooks & Dunn, Tim McGraw, and others.

Paul Worley: Record company executive, record producer, composer, guitarist, arranger, and recording engineer. He is the former vice president of Sony BMG and former chief creative officer at Warner Bros. Records. His recording and production credits include work with Lady Antebellum, Martina McBride, the Dixie Chicks, Sara Evans, Crystal Gayle, Big & Rich, Glen Campbell, Riders in the Sky, Willie Nelson, Hank Williams Jr., Reba McEntire, and others.

Bob Wray: Popular recording session bass guitarist. He has recorded with Dobie Gray, Wilson Pickett, Amy Grant, Roy Orbison, Janie Frickie, B.B. King, and others.

Reggie Young: Guitarist. He was a member of Eddie Bond and the Stompers, the Bill Black Combo, and the Highwaymen with Willie Nelson, Kris Kristofferson, Johnny Cash, and Waylon Jennings. His recording credits include work with Dobie Gray, Jimmy Buffett, Elvis Presley, Ray Stevens, the Oak Ridge Boys, Ernest Tubb, George Jones, Joe Cocker, Reba McEntire, Hank Williams Jr., and others.

Jonathan Yudkin: Multi-instrumentalist (strings), composer, record producer, and arranger. His recording credits include work with Jars of Clay, Suzy Bogguss, Neil Diamond, SHeDAISY, Riders in the Sky, Lonestar, Shania Twain, Rascal Flatts, Martina McBride, Kenny Rogers, Keith Urban, LeAnn Rimes, Sara Evans, Big & Rich, and others.

Saul Zaentz: Oscar-winning film producer, record company executive, and record producer. His film production credits include *One Flew Over the Cuckoo's Nest* and *Amadeus*. He was part owner of Fantasy Records and signed Creedence Clearwater Revival to the record label. His music production credits include albums by Creedence Clearwater Revival, Neville Marriner, John Fogerty, the Mastersounds, and Leonard Rosenman. He was involved in a legal dispute with members of Creedence Clearwater Revival.

Zoro: Drummer, percussionist, and author. He is best known for his work with Lenny Kravitz. He is referred to as "The Minister of Groove." He has also worked with Bobby Brown, the Four Seasons, Sean Lennon, Lisa Marie Presley, and others. He has authored multiple critically acclaimed books, including *The Commandments of Early R&B Drumming* and *The Big Gig*.

INDEX

ABOUT THE AUTHOR

Tony Artimisi has been playing and studying drumming since he was nine years old and is currently assistant professor of music at Winston-Salem State University. His past teachers include Johnny Lee Lane, Ndugu Chancler, Joe Bonadio, Ruben Alvarez, Lewis Nash, John R. Beck, and Glenn Schaft. He earned the degree of Doctor of Musical Arts from the University of North Carolina at Greensboro. His dissertation about Jeff Porcaro inspired him to be proactive about approaching legendary drummers and percussionists to give them opportunities to tell their stories.

Artimisi's other research interests include percussion pedagogy, rhythmic analysis, and music composition. He has articles published by the Percussive Arts Society (PAS) and the Music and Entertainment Industry Educators Association (MEIEA) and has had music published by Row-Loff Publications. He maintains an active recording schedule, presents clinics and master classes, and performs at his church on Sundays.